YOUTH IN CONFLICT
Challenges and Prospects

YOUTH IN CONFLICT

Challenges and Prospects

(A Study of Kashmir)

Bilal Bhat
Aijaz Ashraf

SP SHIPRA
SHIPRA

Rs. 750; US$ 37.50

ISBN: 978-81-7541-812-7

First Published in India in 2016

Youth in Conflict: Challenges and Prospects
A Study of Kashmir

Published by:
SHIPRA PUBLICATIONS
LG 18-19, Pankaj Central Market, I.P. Ext.
Patparganj, Delhi-110092, India
Tel: 91-11-2223 5152, 2223 6152
E-mail: info@shiprapublication.com
www.shiprapublication.com

Preface

Sociologically youth is not only an age category, a period in life, but also a context. It is not merely a biological notion, as for instance puberty. It is rather a sociological concept, representing a system of attitudinal and behavioural patterns related to a specific position in society. This is not to deny the relationship between sociological and biological factors, but merely to distinguish them. Any age category – for instance childhood, youth or old age as in Aristotle's categorization into the three stages of human beings – is predicated upon biological fact, yet is structured by social factors. It is this process of socialization of a given biological group which is so different from moment to moment, society to society, and culture to culture, that gives rise to a set of partially shared perceptions and problems, which among other things contributes to the creation of a common identity. Youth is the generic notion used to describe this common identity. It seeks more specifically sociological criteria and defines youth as a period of transition from childhood to full adult status of full membership in society. In this period, the individual is no longer a child especially from a physical and sexual point of view but is ready to undertake many attributes of an adult and to fulfill the adult roles. But he/she is not acknowledged as an adult, a full member of society. Rather he/she is being 'prepared' or is preparing himself/herself for such adulthood. This definition stresses the place of youth in society as a member, yet not a full member of society. It treats youth as a stage of transition to adulthood, just as infancy gives way to childhood. This view is typically sociological in that it points out that youth should be seen as a product of social reproduction.

The youth are often perceived as agents of social change. This role in social change/transformation is pursued as a result of the young people differentiating between what they accept and what they wish to change in a given social setup, at times through participation in movements for social change. Throughout the world, there have been several cases of such movements by youth. Example can be what was witnessed in the late 1960's, which was marked by the rise of "hippies", who in the West represented a non-violent protest of the youth against western values. They wanted to be left alone to do what they liked without the constraints of the mores and laws of the civilization in which they grew up. The 1970s witnessed the movements of the underprivileged seeking redress of their social disabilities. For example, the Black Panthers of America resorted to militant movements to pursue their goal. An illustration of revolutionary agitation was that of the youth in China in 1987. In India since 1970 there have been a number of cases of youth agitation, such as that of the anti-reservation in Gujarat in 1985, the All Assam Student Union agitation in Assam in 1984 and the anti-Mandal agitation in north India in 1990. The youth have played a part in the militant agitation for Khalistan in Punjab and for an independent Kashmir in Jammu and Kashmir. Furthermore, no less important was the role of youth in the freedom movement in India. Large number of young men and women were actively involved in the freedom struggle under Mahatma Gandhi's leadership. However, it is only in post-independence period that, with the recognition of the existence of youth and youth culture as distinct and separate social entity, youth movement became increasingly the subject matter of academic studies and research works.

Moreover, as in other parts of the country, due to the growing consumerism aggravated by aggressive advertisements there has been a cultural twist also among youth of Jammu and Kashmir. They adopted fashionable concepts of life and want to go beyond old social norms and create their own new world of norms & habits. There appears to be some linkages between the revival of religious fundamentalism on one hand and the growing frustration of general public on the other. Resultantly in this situation a kind of erosion has occurred and the traditions, institutions and cultures that used to keep together individuals in a cohesive society are losing their strength. And before a new form of tradition appears under the new clothes of modernity, people including young people are freed from the ties of the past and left in a no-man's land where norms, hallmarks, signals etc., become blurred and are not able to ensure the relatively better socialization and preparation of the new generation, which in a sense results in emotional tension, a feeling of insecurity and a lack of confidence in ones beliefs and attitudes.

Bilal Bhat
Aijaz Ashraf

Acknowledgements

Particular appreciation, for various combinations of instrumental and expressive assistance, goes to Mr. Yasir Qureshi whose infectious enthusiasm and optimism kept us going and who conceived and steered the programme with indomitable zeal. Mr. Ashfaq Ahmad, Mr. Adil Bashir and Mr. Mohd Aslam from the University of Kashmir also deserve special thanks for their timely help, cooperation and assistance. We thank Inam ul Rehman, Sabeel Kawoosa and Asima Hassan, for taking personal pains while assisting and supporting us for academic and non-academic purposes. We thankfully acknowledge the contribution of our friends and colleagues particularly Javeed, Munir, Shahnawaz, Essar Batool, Shahzad and Nilufar for their spontaneous generosity and empathy. We would like to express our heartfelt gratitude to T.A. Rather, G.N. Khaki and M.A. Mir, Senior Faculty at Centre of Central Asian Studies, University of Kashmir who gave us good initial advice and very helpful introductions. We are thankful to all our interviewees in Rural and Urban Kashmir for their time and willingness to talk with us about their life in the strife-torn Kashmir-valley which enabled us to learn much about their inner life. The unconditional love and sacrifice of our parents has been the fuel and energy for our research and studies. Lastly we record our sincere and grateful thanks to all those authors and writers from whose writings we have been benefitted and take the responsibility for any error and omission.

Contents

Preface v
Acknowledgements ix
List of Tables xiii
List of Figures xiv
Abbreviations xv

1. Introduction **1**

Conceptualizing Youth/6; Growing Up: The Relevance of Age and the Concept of Youth/8; Social Process/13; Popular Conceptions/17

2. Aspirations and Challenges of Youth **23**

Youth as a Problem/26; Rethinking Youth/29; Youth in India/31; Contemporary Youth in Jammu and Kashmir/36

3. Locating Youth in Kashmir **43**

Theoretical Models/Perspectives on Social Problems/43; Using the Theoretical Perspectives/48; Constructing Social Problems/48; Youth in Kashmir/50

4. Analytical Perspective **53**

Relevance and Significance/53; Objectives/54; Politics and Government/65; Tourism/68; Culture/68; Education/69; Policy and Programme Environment/70; Study Phases/71; Study Instruments/73; Study Design and Sample Size/77; Recruitment, Training and Fieldwork/78; Ethical Considerations/79; Data Processing/82

5. Youth and Life Course in Kashmir **83**

Demographic Sketch/85; Age and Sex Composition of Population/86; Education and Opportunity/88; Family,

Friends and Community Life/92; Employment and Unemployment/93; Media Exposure/94; Youth and Mobile Phones/100; Youth and Socialization/102; Peer Group Networks and Interaction/105; Family, Parental Education and Occupation/105; Sex, Gender and Youth/108; Knowledge of Sexual and Reproductive Health Matters/109; Youth, Love Affairs and Romantic Relations/110; Sexual Exploitation and Youth/110; Marriage and Youth/111; Health, Substance/Drug Use and Well Being/113

6. Conflict, Youth and Governance **115**

Youth, Civil Society and Political Engagement/118; Socio-Psychological Impact of Conflict on Youth/122; Socio-Economic Impact of Conflict on Youth/124; Leisure, Conflict and Youth/126; Tourism, Sports and Youth/129; Youth, State and Governance/131

7. Conclusion and Policy Implications **145**

Bibliography **156**

Index **161**

List of Tables

3.1: An Outline of the Sociological Perspectives 49

5.1: Age and Sex Composition of the Sampled Youth 87
5.2: Classification of Sampled Youth by School, College, Education, Profession, Occupation and Area 89
5.3: Classification of Youth According to Activities in Spare Time and Watching Programmes on TV 96
5.4: Preference of Language for Communication in Inside and Outside College/University/Business/School 96
5.5: Preference of Using Languages in Intimate and Formal Correspondences 98
5.6: Preference of Language in Watching TV, Listening Radio and Reading Newspapers and Magazines 99
5.7: Description of Youth Who Believe in the Role of Elders in the Affairs of the Youth 103
5.8: Classification of Youth Who Indicate Separate Image of Theirselves than Adult Society 104
5.9: Family Type and Proficiency in English, Urdu and Kashmiri 106

6.1: Classification of Youth Who have Participated in Any Protest, Demonstration or Movement and Interest in Politics 116
6.2: Classification of Youth on the Basis of Trust on the Institutions of the State/Government 119

6.3: Classification of Youth Who have Casted Votes and Their Belief that Votes have Effect on the Governance and Administration 120
6.4: Classification of Youth on the Basis of Agreement and Disagreement Over the following Statements 121
6.5: Classification of Sampled Youth by Priority to Different Aspects 122
6.6: Description of Insecurity and Anxiety Among Youth 123
6.7: Classification of Youth Experiencing Discrimination on Various Accounts in Day-to-Day Life Within and Outside the State 125
6.8: Description of the Youth Who Believe that Violence can Only Bring Change and Participate in Violence and Strikes 128
6.9: Description of Youth about Panchayat System in Kashmir 129
6.10: Description of Youth Suggesting Aim/Goal of State Government for Next Decade 130

List of Figures

5.1: Most Comfortable Language 97
6.1: 118

Abbreviations

ACCI	Associated Chamber of Commerce and Industry
AFSPA	Armed Forces Special Powers Act
ASB	Amarnath Shrine Board
BJP	Bharatiya Janata Party
HRW	Human Rights Watch
ILO	International Labour Organization
ILRF	International Labour Rights Forum
INC	Indian National Congress
J&K	Jammu and Kashmir
JKNC	Jammu and Kashmir National Conference
KU	Kashmir University
MDG	Millennium Development Goals
MHFW	Ministry of Home and Family Welfare
MYAS	Ministry of Youth Affairs and Sports
NCPCR	National Commission for the Protection of Child Rights
NGO	Non-Government Organization
NYP	National Youth Policy
PDP	Peoples Democratic Party
UN	United Nations
UNDP	United Nations Development Programme
UNESCO	United Nations Educational, Social and Cultural Organization
UNICEF	United Nations Children's Emergency Fund
VK	Valley of Kashmir
YF	Youth Forum
YG	Youth Groups

1
Introduction

Youth as an important age category has been recognized throughout the world and history. The definitions of youth and the concepts people have of the stages in the life of an individual differ from time to time, region to region and culture to culture. There is a considerable variation in the use of the term 'youth' throughout history. For Aristotle and for all antiquity, there were only three ages of man: childhood, youth and old age. In Aristotle's usage 'youth' is any age from about seven to forty or even forty five.[1] Similarly Rousseau, a French scholar is said to have used the term 'youth' as 'young person'.[2]

Unlikely in the traditional Indian context this variation in the concepts of the stages in the life of an individual has to be seen in terms of Brahmanic model. The Brahmanic model for the various stages of life is given by the concept of the four '*Asramas*'[3]... *Brahmacharya, Grihastha, Vanaprastha* and *Sanyasa*. The exact age at which the Stage of *Brahmacharya* began is not fixed and the age at which it ended is not clearly specified though generally the period of serious duty is said to have begun at the age of eight years. It is known that the period of *Brahmacharya* ends when a person enters on the life of a householder a *Grihasta*. Obviously, then the stage of *Brahmacharya* must have extended at least up to the age of eighteen to twenty years. In the terminology of the traditional Indian Society the period of 'youth' is then co-terminus with the stage of *Brahmacharya*—at least for the *Brahmin* and *Brahmanised* caste groups.[4]

Still other societies have their own terms to refer to and conceptualize the stages in the life of an individual. In Arabian societies the term *Murahaqa* is used for adolescence and youth in academic texts, and in common language the terms like *Fata/Fatat (masculine and feminine forms)* or *Shabb/Shabba* are used for young boys and girls respectively which connote marital status or level of responsibility for or obligation to others. These terms also reveal important dimensions of the adolescent period in Arabian societies and capture the laypersons perception of adolescence as loaded with sexual temptations, a period in which adults must closely supervise a young person's activities.[5] Besides, there is the youth orientation in Muslim Societies, which is drawn from the *Holy Quran*. Youth in Islam is perceived as a raw material to be mobilized, brought up and educated. Youth are active and by being active the youth keep youthful.[6]

However speaking sociologically, youth is a special age category, a time of life, but also a context. It is not a biological notion, as for instance puberty is concerned. It is rather a sociological concept: an attitudinal system and a behavioural pattern related to a specific position in society. This is not to deny the relationship between sociological and biological forces, but merely to distinguish them. Any age category—for instance childhood, youth and old age, as Aristotle maintained the three ages of man—is predicated upon biological facts, yet is structured by social forces. It is this process of socialization that is so different from moment to moment, society to society and culture to culture, yet the very fact of socialization upon a given biological group gives rise to a set of partially shared perceptions and problems, which among other things contributes to the creation of a common identity. Youth is the generic notion used to describe this common identity.[7]

To make things more clear, the vast sociological literature on youth comprising the works by sociologists such as E. Erikson, K.L. Allerbeck, E. Spranger, T. Parson, K. Mannheim, Rosenmayr Leopold, J.A. Perez Islas, L. Garrido and S.N. Eisenstadt, describe youth (or adolescence) in a rather formal manner as: a category of chronological age; a segment in the lapse of the individuals life; a stage of psycho-biological development; an element of social replacement; a stage in life marked by incomplete access to social positions; a marginal social category; a constellation of ideologically homogeneous cohorts etc. S.N. Eisenstadt, however, seeks more specifically sociological criteria. He in his book *Archetypical Patterns of Youth* (1972) has defined youth as a "period of transition from childhood to full adult status of full membership in society. In this period, the individual is no longer a child especially from a physical and sexual point of view but is ready to undertake many attributes of an adult and to fulfill the adult roles. But he/she is not acknowledged as an adult, a full member of society. Rather he/she is being 'prepared' or is preparing himself/herself for such adulthood".[8] This definition stresses the place of youth in society as a member yet not a full member of society. Further Eisenstadt looks upon youth as a transition stage. Just as infancy gives way to childhood, youth gives way to adulthood but one step before it. This view is typically sociological in that it stresses that youth should be seen as both a product of social reproduction and a force for social change. These two roles say, social reproduction and social change/ transformation could be pursued as a result of the young people in question differentiating between what they accept and what they wish to change in a given social setup or by replicating patterns of older generation or pursuing a path of social transformation by participating in movements for social change.

In contemporary societies, we have witnessed many such types of movements by youth. Examples can be what we witnessed in the late 1960's, which was marked by the rise of Hippies, who in the West represented the nonviolent protestation of the youth over western values. They want to be left alone to do their thing—to do what they like for as long as they like without the constraints of the mores and laws of the civilization in which they have grown up. Likely closer to 1970's we witnessed the movements of the underprivileged seeking redress for personally felt social disabilities. The Black Panthers of America among Negroes inspired the similar militant movements elsewhere—such as Dalit Panthers among the suppressed and the backward castes in India. Further instances of revolutionary agitation can be illustrated by the youth agitation in China in 1987. In India specifically 1970 onwards number of youth agitations may be cited like the anti-reservation agitation in Gujarat in 1985, the All Assam Students Union agitation in Assam in 1984, the anti-Mandal agitation in north India in 1990. Besides youth played a part in the militant's agitation for Khalistan in Punjab and for an independent Kashmir in Jammu & Kashmir.[9]

Though functional in their own way, all these agitations and protests had some tragic consequences like increasing disorder, mass killing, a reign of terror, smuggling of weapons, criminalization of politics etc. However from this background, Indian youth seem sensible, sensitive, and politically conscious and have a reasonable amount of disillusion with the political class. It is something so obvious in India today-AC-Nielsen-ORG-MARG, 2006, youth survey across 14 cities that 61 per cent respondents between the age-group of 18-35 years of the total sample of 2895 criticized dynastic politics and 88 per cent said that people with criminal records should not be allowed to contest elections. While 84 per cent of youth want uniform civil code, 43 per cent are against religion processions.[10] Hence there seems to be a readiness for religious reforms and a growing attitude towards secularism. Using the well known Marxian Concept, it could be stated that important historical events have to some extent contributed to the transformation of youth from a social category 'in itself' into a category 'for itself' into a social group conscious of its peculiar social conditions, its aspirations and ideology.[11]

However, these are not the only issues concerning contemporary Indian youth. Rather their dissatisfaction with an established social order, expression in shabby dress and non-conformist ideas, art forms and style of life, also arrests the attention of social scientists in general and sociologists in particular. The sociologists who have written on Indian youth generally argue that youth are taking up less responsibility and obligation towards living with old and have expressed problems with aged due to their way of living and behaviour, reflecting the weakness in family structure. For example according to the study entitled, *Views of Youth on the Living Pattern of Elderly,* conducted in the urban areas of 'Kerala', 82 per cent boys and 92 per cent girls between the age group of 21-30 years, criticized over the negative feelings, the elders have over the modern dress worn by youth. The study also reveals that nearly 50 per cent of youth were not happy to spend time with elders as it always ended in clash,[12] because interest in pleasure is stronger for majority of youth than interest in more serious activities. Sex and violence seem to have become two of the major television themes, which offer new examples of behaviour to youth, which they tend to practice in real life. As per the report published in *The Weeks/C-voter,* 2007, 46 per cent respondents between the age-group of 15-19 years of the total sample of 1004, across ten cities of India feel that sex is just for fun. While 61 per cent don't regret losing their virginity, 22 per cent said to have done so by class 12th. Experts who study social trends point to a rise in premarital sex in urban and rural areas. The population council 2006-2007 survey of Maharashtra shows that nearly 14 per cent of urban males have had premarital sex, the figures being 25 per cent for rural male the corresponding figures for females are 11 per cent and 23 per cent of urban and rural areas respectively.[13]

The change sociologists say, is more in the outlook towards these relationships which, consequently has led to the sharp rise in the transmission of HIV/AIDS infection. There were 10 million young people living with this infection in 2005, of this number 6.2 million in Sub-Sahara Africa and 2.2 million in Asia. Globally almost one fourth of those living with AIDS are under the age of 25 years. Particularly in India one fourth of the total estimated 5 million people infected with HIV/AIDS are in the 15-24 age group.[14] Besides there is vulnerability of young people to many other risky behaviours such as excessive alcohol consumption, drug abuse and attempted suicide etc. There is an estimated one billion smokers including heavy drug takers in the world today. Especially in the Central Asia and Eastern Europe up to 25 per cent of those who inject drugs are estimated to be less than 20 years of age.[15] Talking about India, the drug abuse and alcohol consumption is not prevalent in male youth only, the economic independence and changed social environment helped break down of middle class taboos against women drinking and gave emergence to new issues. Women drinkers between the 15-25 age group account for a quarter of the Indian alcohol industries annual 15 per cent growth.[16]

Putting all the pieces together, the broad based empirical generalizations of foregoing enables us to maintain that youth including Indian youth in the current generation come across as both individualistic fun-seekers and frail pragmatists, and I would argue these are the two sides of same coin. Being fun-seekers, it is probably in many cases youth, who are irrational and undisciplined. However and therefore every country needs to pay a great deal of attention to this segment of population, particularly India, which is predominately very young as 38.8 per cent population is between the 10-29 year age group.[17] Because progress of a society depends upon the utilization of youth potential; as Karl Mannheim' in his *Diagnosis of our times*, put forward that, "dynamic societies will rely mainly upon the cooperation of youth."[18] Therefore, this means that ill or good effects on youth are likely to have a long term consequences.

Conceptualizing Youth

Young people in the developed world have been the subjects of an enormous amount of research over the last 40 years. In general, this research assumes that young people constitute a separate and significant category of people: as non-adults. A central and recurring theme in these studies is the problematic nature of being a young person and the even more problematic nature of becoming adult. Much of the literature about youth has inherited assumptions from developmental psychology about universal stages of development, identity formation, normative behaviour and the relationship between social and physical maturation. Yet very little work has been done to clarify the theoretical basis of this categorization based on age.

From time to time this point has been made by youth

researchers. In 1968, Allen argued that the concept of youth needed to be reassessed. She pointed out that, it is not the relations between ages that creates change or stability in society, but change in society which explains relations between different ages (1968, p. 321). Twenty years later, Jones took up the challenge, pointing out that the sociology of youth was yet to develop a conceptual framework for understanding both the transitions young people pass through as they become adult and the different experiences of young people from different social groups. She argued that it is misleading to emphasize the qualities or otherwise of Youth per se, since the young are neither a homogeneous group nor a static one (1988, p. 707). Her conclusion was that youth is most usefully conceptualised as an age-related process. This means that the focus on youth is not on the inherent characteristics of young people themselves, but on the construction of youth through social processes (such as schooling, families or the labour market). Young people engage with these institutions in specific ways, in relation to historical circumstances. There is a growing awareness amongst contemporary youth researchers that focusing on youth as a process throws into question the very use of the universal term youth. For example, recently Liebau and Chisholm (1993) have suggested that European youth do not exist. Their point is that as nationally framed cultures and economies follow their own courses, young people in the different countries and regions that make up Europe negotiate very different circumstances from each other. They are shaped by both the material, objective aspects of the cultures and societies in which they grow up; and by the ways in which they subjectively interpret their circumstances (Liebau & Chisholm 1993, p. 5). Also focusing on young people in European countries, Wallace and Kovacheva (1995) point out that the experience of youth is being de-structured, because the significant transitions in life are less and less age related. They argue that transitions are no longer associated with any age or with each other. Education, for example, has become gradually dissociated from work, and leaving home is not necessarily a transition stage linked with marriage.

The present study will discuss the use and usefulness of the concept of youth the ways in which young people have been conceptualized, examining common assumptions about what growing up means as well as the perspective on the concept of youth as a social process. It is important to study young people because they are embarking on a process involving transitions in many dimensions of life, towards becoming adult and establishing a livelihood. Yet, increasingly, the meaning of adulthood and how it is achieved, marked, acknowledged and maintained is ambiguous. The period of youth is significant because it is the threshold to adulthood, and it is problematic largely because adult status itself is problematic. We will also explore popular conceptions of youth, focusing on the representations of youth in the media as discourses about youth.

Growing Up: The Relevance of Age and the Concept of Youth

One of the most significant issues which confront the area of youth research is the apparent symmetry between biological and social processes. Age is a concept which is assumed to refer to a biological reality. However, the meaning and the experience of age, and of the process of ageing, is subject to historical and cultural processes. Although each person's life span can be measured objectively by the passing of time, cultural understandings about life stages give the process of growing up, and of ageing, its social meaning. Specific social and political processes provide the frame within which cultural meanings are developed. Both youth and childhood have had and continue to have different meanings depending on young people's social, cultural and political circumstances.

Research on young people's lives in non-Western countries exposes the ideal of the happy, safe childhood and period of youth as myths, built around the social preoccupations and priorities of the capitalist countries of Europe and the United States (Boyden, 1990, p. 184). As a stark contrast to the Western ideal, she poses the trafficking and sexual exploitation of children in Thailand and the Philippines, the crimes perpetrated on young people in Argentina under the military regime and the repression and detention of young people in South Africa under apartheid. More importantly, Boyden also refers to ethnographic research which reveals that children and young people are expected to work for an income in some societies (for example, in Bangalore, India), not just for economic reasons, but also because it is believed that they should engage with adult life as early as possible.

When a global perspective is taken, the socially constructed nature of 'youth' becomes more apparent. For a large proportion of the world's young people, the idea of 'youth' as a universal stage of development was and remains an inappropriate concept. In 1986, the International Year of Youth, it was estimated by the International Labour Organisation that globally: there are some 50 million children under the age of 15 who are at work. Nearly 98 per cent of all these child labourers are found in developing countries. The striking increase in the urban youth populations of less developed regions has created the phenomenon of the 'street children' who live and work on the streets, doing anything that will earn them and their families that little extra which enables them to survive. If 'youth' is understood as constituting the period between the end of childhood, on the one hand, and entry into the world of work on the other, then it manifests that youth does not exist in the situations already pointed out (United Nations, 1986, p. 8). Although the experience of youth varies widely, and may not exist at all for some, the concept of youth is important in enabling us to understand some of the complexities of social change and the intersections between institutions and personal biography. We argue that it is most usefully seen as a relational concept, which refers to the social processes whereby age is socially constructed, institutionalized and controlled in historically and culturally specific ways. It may be useful here to refer to earlier conceptual debates over the concept of gender, because there are similarities. In the 1960s and 1970s, the idea of sex roles was especially powerful in drawing attention to inequalities between men and women.

The concept of sex roles provided a framework in which both men and women were seen to become limited by socially constructed categories, or roles. Although this concept offered a useful descriptive model, and was a significant basis for educational strategies to address gender inequality (Connell, 1987), it had serious drawbacks. The static and categorical concept of sex roles, in which masculinity and femininity were seen as simply discrete, if socially constructed, categories failed to give any grasp of the relationship between masculinities and femininities. Ultimately, the sex roles framework was replaced by a more sophisticated understanding of gender as a relational concept, which placed power at the centre. Gender as a relational concept draws attention to the ways in which masculinity and femininity are constructed in relation to each other. They are not simply 'different' categories and they cannot be understood independently of each other. Davies, for example, describes how the boys in her study worked hard to maintain a dualism between 'boys' and 'girls' by denigrating, devaluing and constantly drawing attention to 'feminine' behaviour. These boys provide an example of the way in which 'being masculine' involves maintaining a hierarchy in which being male has the greater value (Davies, 1993, p. 107). There are several useful discussions of this conceptual issue; for example, Franzway and Lowe (1978), Connell (1987) and Edwards (1983) have provided extensive analyses of the limitations of a categorical approach to gender relations.

Youth is a relational concept because it exists and has meaning largely in relation to the concept of adulthood. The concept of youth, as idealised and institutionalised (for example in education systems and welfare organisations in industrialised countries) supposes eventual arrival at the status of adulthood. If youth is a state of 'becoming', adulthood is the 'arrival'. At the same time, youth is also 'not adult', a deficit of the adult state. This dimension of the concept of youth is evident in the positioning of young people as requiring guidance and expert attention (from professionals) to ensure that the process of becoming adult is conducted correctly.

Understanding youth as a relational concept brings power

relations to the forefront. For the purposes of our analysis, this is an important dimension in understanding the experiences that different groups of young people have of growing up. The popular image of young people presenting a 'threat' to law and order represents young people as more powerful than they really are. Although young people have 'rights' as young citizens, these are relatively easily denied, and they have very little say in the institutions in which they have the most at stake, such as education.

Another similarity between the conceptualization of gender as relations of power (through the constructions of masculinities and femininities) and age (through the constructions of youth and adulthood) is that both involve interpretations of physical or biological 'realities'. The challenge, in rethinking youth, is to maintain a balance between recognizing the importance of physical and psychological changes which occur in young people's lives and recognizing the extent to which these are constructed by social institutions and negotiated by individuals. Importantly, it is also necessary to understand the extent to which categorical conceptions of youth have been central to denying young people their rights by creating frameworks within which adults can judge some young people as 'normal' and others as in need of intervention.

We would characterize approaches to youth which are based primarily on age groupings as categorical. The concept of adolescence epitomizes this approach, because it assumes the existence of essential characteristics in young people because of their age, focusing on the assumed link between physical growth and social identity. For example, adolescence is assumed to involve a number of developmental tasks which must be completed appropriately or the young person will not develop into a fully mature adult.

One of the limitations of taking a categorical approach to the study of youth is the historical and static nature of this approach. The assumption that age is the central feature characterising young people gives insufficient weight to difference, process and change. A categorical approach tends to rest on the assumption that the similarities amongst the age category are more significant than the differences, taking masculine, white, middle class experience as the norm. It offers little grasp of the ways in which the experience of growing up is a process, negotiated by young people as well as being imposed on them.

A categorical approach also ignores the significant role of institutions and of changing economic and political circumstances and their impact on youth. The result is the tendency to present the attitudes, behaviours and styles of particular groups as normative and to underestimate diversity amongst young people. Furthermore, this approach takes little or no account of the relations between young people and adults (for example, in communities where there is high unemployment, in rural communities during recession, within elite families or in urban Aboriginal communities). It also tends to ignore the relations between groups of young people. Schooling, for example, structures competition between groups of young people in classrooms, as young people learn their 'place' in the hierarchy of performance. Relations between groups of young people are also structured through schooling systems. The privatisation of education also carries the message that some schools (and by implication, their students) are 'better' than others. In some states of Australia, where a large private education sector is well established, young people in private schools learn quite explicitly that they are an elite (Davies, 1993; Kenway, 1990).

In addition, a static approach to the study of youth as a category overlooks the continuities linking past, present and future. This shortcoming has the potential to be addressed in contemporary research that takes a 'life course' approach to studying issues such as transition from school to work. Kruger (1993) for example, demonstrates that a focus on youth alone may obscure significant continuities between generations of women, by looking at life stages in isolation from one another. A further dimension of the links between past, present and future is the positioning of youth (and childhood) as a reference point for future 'real' life. Youth is seen as a separate 'stage' of life because the time of youth is about preparation for future (real) life, adulthood. Although this dimension would seem to contradict the static nature of approaches to the study of youth, when used uncritically it reinforces the idea that young people are marginal members of society, awaiting their full participation when they reach adulthood. The tendency to emphasise the qualities of 'youth' per se has been especially strong within the tradition of developmental psychology, which has influenced conceptions of youth which are used more broadly.

Social Process

There are many ways in which growing up in the 1990s in the industrialised world is fundamentally different from in the 1950s. It is important to ask, what are the circumstances under which particular groups of young people make the transitions to adulthood? Although the concept of youth as a subject of research was associated with social conditions prevailing in developed countries following the Second World War (Frith, 1986), it is argued that youth as a period of transition into adulthood has a much longer history. Indeed, a focus on youth has a history extending back much further, depending on how youth is defined. For example, during the late nineteenth century and early twentieth century, working class youth were regularly portrayed as a public problem, and besides regular media coverage, were the subject of sustained academic and government study (Finch, 1993).

Mitterauer (1993) further argues that it is too simplistic to assume, because of linguistic evidence alone, that the period of youth did not exist in Europe prior to the seventeenth century. His study explores the possible bases for categorising youth, clearly demarcating between childhood and adulthood. He explores the historical validity of five 'transitions in status': leaving school, finding employment, leaving home, setting up home and marriage. Mitterauer concludes that youth, as a period of transition to adulthood is not usefully categorised in this way, because the timing of these aspects of transition, their meaning and their order of occurrence differ for young men and young women, and from one region to another, reflecting urban, rural differences as well as regional economic differences.

The analysis of traditional thresholds of youth has shown that many of them were applicable only to young men. This was particularly true of thresholds which had their historical roots in the granting of arms. Like these traditional thresholds, the concepts of youth which are based on them are primarily male in orientation. Male and female youth were so different that until the end of the nineteenth century the concepts relating to the age-group were entirely gender specific. Only then did a sexually inclusive collective concept of youth emerge. But even so, the turning points of the biography of youth continued to be very different for the two sexes (Mitterauer, 1993 p. 87).

Youth, as a period of transition to adulthood, has meaning only in relation to the specific circumstances of social, political and economic conditions. Once this is understood, it is possible to bring social conditions to the foreground and examine the significant differences between groups of young people as they engage with the processes which will take them closer to adult life. Inevitably, viewing youth as a social process raises questions about the meaning of 'adult' status. For the concept of youth to have meaning its end point, adulthood, also has to have a clear meaning.

Historically, there have been periods when, for some groups of young people, the social processes were far clearer than they are today. For example, becoming adult for middle class male Australians in the 1960s was largely a process of getting a job, a car, establishing a career, getting married and buying a home. For this group, as for white middle class men in most developed countries at this time, youth and adulthood were relatively clearly demarcated by accepted patterns of consumption and production. The concept of youth as a distinct category, within a finite time span, fits the experiences of this historical group most closely.

Even during this time, however, the patterns of growing up on which the concept is based were not universally experienced. The transitions to adulthood for women were very different from their male counterparts. Women's patterns of employment did not match men's. They were much more likely to remain dependent on a partner or on the government if they were the recipients of income security. Women in the paid workforce were largely ignored by trade unions and by government policy (Probert, 1989). It was only in the latter half of the 1960s that Europe and Australia women, upon marriage, were not required to resign their permanent positions as teachers. Their participation in the workforce, although increasing, revealed that women were limited to employment in a few sectors of the labour market compared with men, and they were not represented in the higher paid, senior positions of their occupations. These examples illustrate that the concept of youth involves a tension between the social significance of age, which gives young people a common social status which is different from adulthood, and the social significance of other social divisions, which differentiate young people from each other.

While young people do have a common status and to some extent common experiences (for example, schooling) because of their age, there are many 'forces which work against this. For example, researchers are now beginning to provide evidence that the experiences of older people in the labour market and in the home have a strong impact on the visions young people have of their own futures. This means that gender divisions and inequalities continue to have a powerful impact on the way in which young men and women approach the decisions which will affect their futures. Young women accept that it is possible for women to challenge the occupational boundaries of the gender-segmented labour market, but many are reluctant to do so, because they envisage their futures as adults in terms of balancing paid and unpaid labour and public and private responsibilities (Ashenden & Associates, 1992).

Researchers in Canada, the Netherlands and Germany have found the same trends occurring with regard to young women's approaches to adult life (Looker, 1993; du Bois-Reymond *et al.* 1994; Kruger, 1993). Young women, even though they might be aware of the potential opportunities that education offers them to achieve 'equality' with their male peers, continue to make decisions about their futures based on what they perceive to be the reality, that is, inequality. In Australia, young Aboriginal people of both sexes in the 1960s also anticipated a very different transition to adulthood from their white counterparts. Even in the 1980s, the relevance of the term 'adolescence' for young Aboriginal people was contested. McConnochie (1982) argues that the category of youth, as employed by many non-indigenous researchers, is inappropriate to characterise the social experience of growing up for young Aboriginal people. McConnochie's reservation about the use of the term 'adolescence' stemmed from his perception that it implied that there were 'internal psychological traits' which could be used to explain behaviour. By contrast he pointed to the nature of the social conditions affecting many young Aboriginal people. Traditional Aboriginal cultures carefully prescribed the process of becoming an adult, leaving relatively little room for speculation. However, fundamental social change to the traditional life of Aboriginal peoples meant that both achieving adult status and the meaning of adulthood have become increasingly ambiguous and uncertain.

The idea that youth only has meaning in relation to specific circumstances is also supported by a consideration of class relations. One of the key conditions that young people have had to face during the 1980s and 1990s is the failure of the economies of most Western societies to provide employment that sustains the establishment of a legitimate livelihood for significant proportions of young people. The struggle to establish a livelihood, historically the special burden of working class communities, continues to be central (Wilson & Wyn, 1987). In the 1990s, it is clear from the experience of New Zealand that economic growth can continue to produce jobs and improve the standard of living of a proportion of the population, while at the same time the conditions and life chances of a large proportion of the society can actually deteriorate (Kelsey, 1995). Young people who fail to find employment that is stable enough and well paid enough to establish a legitimate livelihood have major difficulties now and in later life. These young people become marginal to our society not because of their youth, but because of the operation of economic and political processes. There is increasing evidence that activities across multiple economies is the only way young people can gain access to a livelihood that is sustaining, if not legitimate.

On a global scale, social and economic changes which affect remote, small-scale and large urban communities alike have a significant impact on the meaning and experience of 'growing up'. Although the impact of these changes is far reaching, it does not mean that the outcomes for young people are all the same. As this discussion has begun to point out, the social processes which affect the experience of growing up serve to differentiate groups of young people from each other, sharpening and reinforcing deeper social divisions rather than breaking them down. This discussion of social process has attempted to outline some of the issues that the processes of social change raise for a conceptualization of youth.

Popular Conceptions

Our discussion of the concept of youth would be incomplete without a consideration of the contribution of popular conceptions. The idea that youth constitutes a significant and distinct category is inevitably reinforced by popular media. Indeed, the analysis of media representations of young people occupies a distinct place within youth research. It is widely argued that in the 1950s, as patterns of consumption and production changed to give groups of working class young men greater leisure time and more buying power, the popular media (mainly newspapers) were involved in the presentation of particular constructions of young people (mostly young working class men). The term 'youth' became widely used in the 1950s in industrialised countries, as the experience of growing up responded to changing economic and political processes.

Frith (1986) argues that the term 'youth' was initially most frequently used in research on young men from working class backgrounds, mainly in the United States and in Britain. Relatively high rates of employment gave this group unprecedented disposable income, enabling them to use their leisure time in new ways, and giving them both a visibility and a form of power (Stratton, 1993). Youth became a 'new category' of person, distinctive, usually male, and a potential threat to the stability of society. Although the sense of threat implied physical threat, there was also a sense in which young people were seen to symbolize change to moral and cultural values as well. This sense of threat was described by Cohen (1972) as precipitating 'moral panics' about the violent or disruptive behaviour of youth.

Historical analyses of the popular representations of young people in Australia before the 1950s, however, suggest that it is important to recognise the continuity of popular discourses about youth. In contrast to the historical evidence of considerable diversity in young people's lives, several themes in popular conceptions of youth have dominated. Bessant (1993) has summed up these themes in a recent discussion of the 'cultures' of young Australians in the years between 1900 and 1950. She discusses the dual popular representations of young people: as threat and inherently bad; and at the same time as the focus of hope and optimism and intrinsically good but vulnerable. This discourse rested, Bessant argues, on the assumption that young people were naturally rather animalistic and uncontrollable, but that if tamed by social conventions they could be respectable. The assumption of this dual representation (of which the more negative image was dominant), provided an ongoing legitimation for state intervention, control and protection. As many researchers have pointed out, the youth who were represented in this way were almost exclusively male. These discourses also both drew on and fed the newly developing psychological theories which assumed that young people needed to pass through a series of developmental stages in which they defied the conventions of society and experienced a time of storm and stress, emerging from this process and having found themselves.

Subsequent analyses of later post-1950s popular conceptions of youth in the media reveal continuity with these early discourses. Newspaper articles on youth are inevitably about young working class men (and often, especially indigenous and ethnic minority youth) who are seen as a threat to the assumed values of a 'majority', because of their style of dress, their violent behaviour, their drug-taking behaviour, or because of their attitudes towards employment, schooling or political processes. Stratton's (1993) analysis of the media treatment of young people in the 1950s, for example, argues that the derogatory portrayal of young people as 'Bodgies and Widgies' was a dominant theme. As the analyses of these media representations point out, it is seldom revealed that the young people who are represented in this way constitute a small proportion of the young population.

In addition to being portrayed as a threat, youth are represented in the media as both symbols and victims of modern society. In her analysis of girlhood in the 1950s, Johnson explores this theme, arguing that the concept of youth provided the imagery for it as a time of uncertainty, which although threatening because of its potential to disrupt, would be prescribed by the biological processes of growing up, leading naturally to a stage of greater stability and certainty in adulthood (Johnson, 1993, p. 36). The insights of developmental psychology offered a perspective on youth as a time of turmoil and change, in which adulthood was reached after completing specific normative tasks such as identity formation.

Johnson (1993) has also argued that the masculine bias in the concept of youth derives in part from the significance that youth had in the 1950s and 1960s as a symbol of the emerging post-war, virile and self-determined economies and societies of the developed world. The fit between this imagery and the experience of white middle class young people at that time was close enough to maintain the myth, with the promise that the transition from youth into a secure and certain adulthood would also be the process for working class males. Johnson's analysis offers a useful perspective on the use of the concept of youth in Australia in the 1950s. However, what is the symbolism of youth in the 1990s? Now, the transition into adulthood is into a world of widespread uncertainty and scarcity. Young people in the 1990s are seen to face significantly different circumstances from those of previous generations. Giroux, writing specifically about young people in the United States, suggests that 'plurality and contingency' either mediated through 'media culture' or the economic system, have resulted in a world with few secure psychological, economic, or intellectual markers (1994, p. 287). For Giroux, young people are: condemned to wander within and between multiple borders and spaces marked by excess, otherness and difference. This is a world in which old certainties are ruptured and meaning becomes more contingent, less indebted to the dictates of reverence and established truth. While the circumstances of youth vary across and within terrains marked by racial and class differences, the modernist world of certainty and order that has traditionally policed, contained, and insulated such difference has given way to a shared postmodern culture in which representational borders collapse into new hybridized forms of cultural performance, identity and political agency (1994, pp. 287-88).

Giroux's analysis suggests that popular conceptions of youth in the media not only represent youth, but actively construct the experience and meaning of youth, offering a frame of reference that may replace traditional frameworks. In the 1990s, we argue, popular conceptions of youth continue to portray the dualism of young people as both the symbol of society's future and its victims, 'at risk' of succumbing to lives of violence, drug dependence and moral degeneracy. In the 1990s, the symbolic representation of youth lies in the areas described by Giroux above as 'cultural performance, identity and political agency'. Instead of symbolizing the certainty of reaching the defined status of adulthood, youth in the 1990s, as portrayed in popular conceptions, symbolizes the use of new forms of consumption. For those who can afford them, the technologies are now available to modify, shape or transform the body; so that young people can become 'perfect' and old people can look young. 'Youth' now has symbolic value as the 'outcome' of the process of becoming more and more in control over one's body.

The changing symbolic representation of youth has meaning and value in an increasingly global way, in a world in which traditional boundaries are eroded. The traditional markers of the end of youth are less and less meaningful. The implication of this is that youth as a social experience can be continuously available, regardless of age, the 'becoming' can go on and on. Youth, then, has symbolic meaning as an item of consumption. Of course, this symbolic representation of youth does not mean that everyone, or even a majority of people experience this. It is enough for highly visible media personalities to keep coming back, 'younger' than they were the first time around.

'Youth' as a symbol of consumption does, in a paradoxical way challenge the concept of youth as an age category. This emerging meaning of 'youth' means 'appearance', rather than age as such. The symbolic value of the concept of youth in the 1990s, then, is of youth as the future of society, not in the sense of the 1950s when coming to maturity was the imagery, but in the sense of having access to the trappings of youth throughout life, through consumption, and through performance. The symbolic meaning of youth, then, is not 'coming of age', but 'being anything you want to be'. In addressing the question of what is the symbolism of youth in the 1990s, it is apparent that, as in previous eras, there are a number of dimensions which are simultaneous. At the same time that the concept of youth is an emerging symbol of consumption in society, young people continue to be presented as victims and therefore as a problem.

Notes

1. Yedla S.C., 1989, *Youth in the Contemporary World,* New Delhi: Mittal Publications. p. ix.
2. D.K. Misra and M. Jain, 1975, *Youth, University and Community,* New Delhi: S. Chand & Company, p. 9.

3. *Ashramas*—Stages in the progress through life. *Vanaprastha* is the stage when the house holder, having discharged his duties, retires to the forest, preparatory to renunciation of worldly goods. In 'Sanyasa' he renounces all possessions except his loin cloth, begging bowl and water pot and lives by begging.
4. M.S. Gore, 1977, *Indian Youth: Processes of Socialization,* Vishwa Yuvak Kendra New Delhi, pp. 4-5.
5. B. Bradford, R. Larson and Saraswathi T.S., 2002. *The World's Youth: Adolescence in Eight Regions of the Globe,* Cambridge University Press, pp. 4-6.
6. Yedla S.C, 1989, *Op. cit.,* p. xiii.
7. United Nations Publication New York, 1986, *The Situation of Youth in the 1980's and Prospects and Challenges for the Year 2000,* pp. 10-11.
8. S.N. Eisenstadt, 1972, *Archetypical Patterns of Youth, cit.,* in P.K. Manning and Marcello. T. (eds.) *Youth and Sociology,* Englewood Cliffs, New Jersey, Prentice Hall, Inc. cit., from Kohli A.S. and Narala. V. (eds.) *Youth in Planned Development in India,* 'Social Change: Issues and Perspectives'. June 2004, vol. 34, No. 2, pp. 103-104.
9. Ram Ahuja, 1997, *Social Problems in India,* 2nd (eds.), Rawat Publications, Jaipur, pp. 193-216.
10. *India Today,* Feb. 20, 2006, pp. 12-57.
11. J.A Ponsioen, 1966, *The situation of youth in a changing society,* Institute of Social Studies, The Hague, p. 9.
12. S. Royse and Celia Verghese, *Social Welfare,* July 2007, vol. 54, No. 4, pp. 33-36.
13. *The Week,* September 16, 2007, pp. 32-43.
14. UN Report on Global Aids Epidemic, 2005, Geneva, cit., in Potdar Rukmini and Koenig A. Michael, *Does Audio–CASI Improve* Reports *of Risky Behaviour? Evidence from a Randomized field trial among Young Urban men in India,* June 2005, Population council publication Studies in family Planning, vol. 36, No. 2, pp. 107-116.
15. UN Aids and Development Cooperation', Ireland, *Loc. Cit.,* Lopez P.R., Future World Wide Health Effects of Current Smoking, cit., in Koop E.C. and R.M. Shwarz (eds.) *Initial issues in Global Health,* 2001, San Franciso, pp. 56-85.
16. *Out Look,* The Weekly News Magazine, 27 May-2 June, 2008, pp. 51-64.
17. Subhash Joshi, 2006, *Children Youth and Electronic Media: Prospects and Portents,* B.R. Publishing Corporation India, pp. 3-6.
18. Karal Mannheim, 1943, Diagnosis of our Times, p. 33, cit., in Lakshmi Narayana, H.D. (eds.) 1985, *College Youth Challenge and Response,* Mittal Publications New Delhi, pp. 3-6.

2
Aspirations and Challenges of Youth

The historical and theoretical background of literature on youth can be well traced at least as far back as August Comte's *'Positive Philosophy'*. In the fourth volume of *'Positive Philosophy Lecture 51'*, he put forward a hypothesis according to which the rate of change in society was related to the succession of generations: "The shorter the life-span of a generation, the more forceful the social change."[1] This hypothesis was disproved by the course of social and demographic developments in twentieth century. It may however, be regarded as the first important contribution to the sociology/sociological theory of youth. This hypothesis makes it clear that youth is a factor of social change: not because it is subjected to the socializing influence of the adult institutions and a stage in formation of social identity. Besides youth is an important element in the process of historical development and of cultural change/ transformation. August Comte was contended that youth is endowed with the 'instincts of change'. And as a positivist his ideal of progress was related to the positive evaluation of youth and opposed the tradition-oriented conservative forces. But at the same time, he was very much critical of the disruptions of social order.

Specifically at the beginning of the twentieth century, G.S. Hall's theory of personality development started a trend of psychological and socio-psychological studies focused on adolescence as a special subject of research. He introduced this new term *'ADOLSCENCE'* in his book *'On Adolescence' in (1904).*

His main arguments, however, were culture bonded, class bonded and philosophical rather than scientific, and are representing the reflections of evolutionary theorists.

Although individual historical, literary or ethnological studies of youth culture phenomena were conducted early on with a certain amount of parallel discussions from a psychoanalytical vantage point, it was in the 1960's that a more comprehensive and diversified treatment of youth cultural forms and activities appear and was developed in several countries.[2] J.S. Coleman's research report in his book *Adolescent Society* (1961) was in some way considered comprehensive research report limited to one problem and based on one questionnaire. Because of the vast array of research techniques used in this research, it was for a long time considered most remarkable approach in western sociological literature on youth and adolescents.

However in the 'Worlds Tenth Congress of Sociology' (1982) in Mexico, there had been a presentation of documents regarding youth movements and held youth as the *nineteen sixties global generation.* But this statement was not applicable world-wide because, there were differences in the life conditions of young people in different parts of the world. And such differences were brought out in the same congress about the Indian village youth and Japanese youth from vocational orientation centre and about frustrated Moroccan boys in Dutch cities. Besides this, in a paper from UNESCO various differences in the context of Asia were alone presented on the mobilization of Asian youth for social activity and development.[3]

The international youth year (1985) was an attempt to end these differences and fragmentation in identifying, conceptualizing and attempting solutions to the specific problems of young people. The concept of youth became very much a part of international discourse and the international development strategy for the third United Nations Development decade recommended that all countries should give priority to the mobilization and integration of youth in development,[4] which in turn sharpened the designation of (1985) as international youth year.[5]

However, till recently, in reality there were still differences in the situation and conditions of youth in different parts of the world. For example the book entitled, *The World Youth: Adolescence in eight regions of the globe,* 2002.[6] The book in its totality is a remarkable attempt by an international team of scholars, to comment on the youth of eight regions of the world. To begin with, the book reveals that there is absorption, assimilation and influence coming from the globalization process, but it is not uniform. The more the world globalizes, the more gaps between countries or regions increase; inequalities are becoming apparent within societies as well. The authors maintain that people speak of the emergence of a *global youth culture* and view that youth wear the same clothing and hair style, listen to some of the same music, share same challenges, interest and concerns, but in reality differences of the situations of youth and of the frames that contribute to the shaping of their lives remain strengthened. In Arab societies strong traditional system of family relationship is operating, religion is strong and governs the actions and behaviour of young people. Obedience to fathers and elders is almost unquestionable. Similarly in China and Japan, there are strong family centered traditions and family honour remains crucial motivation to young people in their educational and carrier choices etc. where as in the Western and European countries, greater openness and weakening authority of parents may contribute to the relatively higher rates of deviant behaviour that characterize several North American societies as well. Similarly these societies as described in this book display differences in their response to the role of peer groups in socialization and development of the youth. Opportunities for peer interactions are severely limited in Arab states, especially for girls. Where as in Africa, North America and Europe, however in some cases peer groups play like substitute families. Particularly in chapter six, authors link the increased rates of sexual activity among South Asian youth to decreased parental supervision resulting from mother's employment and young people's migration to cities for employment. Further the book reveals that in India, Latin America, Southeast Asia and Arab societies, sexual adventures among boys is tolerated to some extent, but in same societies opportunities for girls to develop romantic and sexual relations are restricted. Furthermore it also talks about the exploitation of youth in Latin America, Arab, Africa and Southeast Asia, where youth are forced to participate in armed conflicts and wartime. On the other hand authors describe how Russian youth benefit from the transformation of their society from a communist to democratic state. Besides, the book also reveals that there is an increase in the rates of HIV infection among youth of many underdeveloped and developing countries. Thus all these situations and conditions of youth lives, identified, evaluated and discussed by authors from different regions of the world in this book prevents us from considering that there is a single new generation, rather this generation is made of worlds that have almost nothing to share. And hence one must look closely to identify the challenges that young people face in twenty first century.

Youth as a Problem

The idea that youth are a problem to society, and to themselves, is a central theme to which the media and youth researchers alike return. One dimension of popular conceptions of youth in the media involves the positioning of young people as a threat to accepted social values, and as likely to engage in risky behaviours.

Historical analyses of the youth as a problem approach, although acknowledging that it goes back to the turn of the century or earlier, usually focus on the 1950s, seeing this as a time when both media and social researchers treated the phenomenon as if it were new. The new interest in young people as troublesome is often linked to the changing economic and social conditions and circumstances, and their impact on working class youth. In his succinct treatment of the sociology of youth, Frith (1986) argues that the increased affluence of working class youth created new modes of consumption, of leisure, and of distinctive styles of clothing and music, which were identified with youth culture.

At the same time, the concept of juvenile delinquents came into use. Johnson's discussion of troublesome youth provides a useful summary of juvenile delinquency as a set of concerns about the activities of young people and their supervision by institutions or individuals representing the social order (1993, p. 96). What Johnson's analysis makes clear is the integral link between development of a discourse of youth as a problem, and the establishment of many levels of institutions and processes for the monitoring, processing and surveillance of young people. While these institutions (schools, social welfare organizations and the juvenile justice system, for example) were increasingly charged with a responsibility for young people, this role was seen to be complementary to and possibly in support of family life. However, signs of failure to develop appropriately were to be dealt with by interventions of experts in the lives of children or their parents. The monitoring of young people has inevitably led to the idea that some young people can be identified as at risk (of a variety of things, including not developing through the assumed stages of adolescence properly or failing school). This concept plays a key role in positioning young people as a problem. It is assumed that not all young people are a problem, only a group who are not growing up in the way that they should. This problem group is identified as different in identifiable ways from an assumed mainstream of young people, either in terms of psychological characteristics (such as learning difficulties) or social characteristics (for example, young people from single-parent families). The concept of 'at risk' depends on the idea that a majority of young people are on target, making the transitions towards adulthood in the appropriate way. The concept of 'at risk' and its corollary, the idea of a mainstream, are central to a categorical approach to conceptualizing youth. The assumption that an identifiable group of young people are at risk gives credibility to the notion, integral to most education systems, that all other young people are by and large the same. The idea that some young people are at risk is also central to one of the dimensions of youth as a problem, the idea that youth are victims of society, as well as a threat to it. In the last decade, the newly found affluence of working class youth has been replaced by the poverty of communities who are bearing the brunt of economic restructuring. With the virtual disappearance of traditional youth labour markets, young people who would rather get a job are refugees in education systems which were never intended to address these people's approaches to life or to education and which cannot deliver their promise of access to a better life. Recently, this approach has re-emerged with the idea that the young are a lost generation (Daniel & Cornwall 1993). Daniel and Cornwall's study of young people focuses on disadvantaged young people, presenting their perspectives on work, school and youth services. The picture which emerges from this study is of a group of young people who have few points of engagement with society, and feel that they do not belong. This group of young people were portrayed as a 'lost generation', not because of their own behaviours or characteristics, but because they were the victims of changes to and developments in the economic and social organization of Australian society, which marginalized them. The concept of a youth 'underclass' is also gaining currency as a concept which describes the victim status of young people who are marginalized from society. Some writers focus on this group from the point of view of behaviour, arguing that young people themselves, through antisocial attitudes and activities, are a threat to society. Others argue that the notion of an underclass is useful because it highlights the marginalization of young people by society.

Both concepts of lost generation and youth underclass, although useful in drawing attention to the plight of some groups of young people, do so at the risk of sensationalizing their situation. Both concepts are descriptive, collecting together groups of young people who have been marginalized from the major benefits and institutions of society, emphasizing the hopelessness of the situation of this group, and at the same time rendering invisible the differences amongst them. Critics of the concept of a youth underclass argue that it is too broad a concept to generate an understanding of the marginalizing processes, focusing instead on the results of marginalization (Williamson, 1995). This means that although the concept is useful in pointing out the severity of some young people's circumstances, it does not provide the basis for an analysis that would enable their situation to be addressed. For example, although they are both marginalized, it is not useful to place in the same category black teenage mothers with young white men in rural communities in the United States, because their marginalization can only be seen as the same in the broadest possible terms. Although the effects may be seen as marginalization, the processes creating these outcomes are very different, and their routes towards gaining an adequate livelihood are likely to be very different.

Rethinking Youth

The construction of youth as victims and as vulnerable was challenged by the emerging cultural studies research traditions which suggested that young people were not necessarily passive 'victims' of society. During the 1970s cultural analysis of young people emerged as a strong influence on thinking about youth. This tradition explored the dynamic relationship between particular groups of young people and forms of popular culture, including dress (style), music, film and video (Hall & Jefferson, 1976).

The detailed ethnographic studies of groups of young working class men which were generated at this time were informed by a perspective that highlighted the active participation of these young people in negotiating their lives, albeit within the boundaries of their communities. At the time, the concept of resistance offered a view of these young working class men as agents rather than as recipients of a dominant culture. In some of these works, the emphasis was on their engagement in class relations, rather than on age as such (Hall & Jefferson, 1976). Others argued that it was necessary to examine the relations between class and age, and particularly the way in which age is a mediator of class relations (Murdoch &McCron, 1976, p. 10). However, despite this, the studies emerging from this tradition have tended to give visibility to the practices, styles and perspectives of young men, and later, young women, reinforcing their 'difference' from 'adult society' (Taylor, 1993). This tradition of ethnographic research on young people has also provided a perspective on the way in which groups of young people take up popular media, not as mindless consumers, but as an expression of their resistance to the dominant culture. Many studies have presented the practices of young people in terms of sub-cultural styles of expression, which, in their everyday lives, subvert aspects of the dominant culture (Hall & Jefferson, 1976).

However, critics have pointed out that the focus on the relationship of young people to popular culture has tended to underplay the historically specific nature of this relationship. The meaning of 'the dominant culture', the extent to which it is contested and the form this takes are related to social divisions such as gender, ethnicity and race. The expression of youthful self that is evident in the adoption of popular music by young Aboriginal people in remote Australian communities (Brady, 1992) has very different meanings and implications from its use by middle class white young women in Brisbane (Gilbert & Taylor, 1991).

Johnson (1993) argues that in taking insufficient account of the different expressions and meanings of the relationship of young people to popular culture, the cultural studies approach has taken for granted the idea that young people have a pre-social self which they strive to develop and express through their engagement with mass media. By 'pre-social' self she means an 'essential' self, which exists independently of social relationships, and which will strive to gain expression. Hence, although the cultural studies tradition offered an approach in which young people's behaviour was seen as constructive rather than problematic, in some of its manifestations it failed to challenge the categorical concept of youth.

The central issue is the contradiction that young people

do share in common their age, but the social, economic and cultural significance of this physical reality is far from common. The literature outlines the argument, which forms the framework, that a relational concept of youth offers an approach to understanding the social meaning of growing up that can take account of the diverse ways in which young people are constructed through social institutions, and the ways in which they negotiate their transitions. This approach problematizes the meaning of adulthood, a status which is generally taken for granted in discussions of youth and youth transitions and development.

There are many studies of young people which offer insights into the multiple and diverse experiences of growing up. Perhaps overwhelmed by the dominance of the developmental psychological approach to youth (youth development), few have explored the implications of challenging the categorical approach to youth research, youth studies and to youth policy. There is dire need to study, debate and discuss such a challenge, drawing on our own and others, research to 'rethink youth', and to develop a framework for researching young people's experiences of growing up.

Youth in India

The emergence of youth as a major force in national movements in various parts of the world is a significant phenomenon of the twentieth century. No less important was the role of the youth in the freedom movements particularly in Asia. In India a large number of young men and women were actively involved in the freedom struggle under Gandhi's leadership. However, it is only in post-independence period which is marked by an increasing focus of academic studies and research works on youth with an increasing recognition of the existence of youth and youth culture as distinct and separate entity from adult society. There has been considerable attempt by social scientists to empirically identify the different aspects, conditions and problems concerning Indian youth with special reference to their educational and occupational aspirations, their values and attitudes, culture and subculture etc. In order to have some sort of better understanding of the sociological literature on Indian youth. Some of these studies mainly started in early sixties are critically evaluated here.

This study *"She Who Rides the Peacock: Indian students and social change"* by Margaret Cormack in 1961 is all about to evaluate awareness and attitude of Indian college and university students towards social change and modernization in India. The study particularly focuses on the changing attitude of both male and female youth towards marriage, type of marriage, mate-selection, husband and wife relationship and their attitudes towards becoming modern. Yet the change is very limited. For this study a sample of five hundred male and female youth from different universities were selected. Although there are some methodological inconsistencies in this study; like having voluntary respondents about which the author herself has mentioned and which don't enable her to generalize about any one particular group, the study undoubtedly generates several theoretical formulations which need to be validated through much needed scientific research in this very important area.

'Social change and college students of Gujarat', a study by B.V. Shah in 1964 reveals to some extent similar kind of facts as the above ones. The main areas probed were the type of family, caste endogamy, boy-girl relationships, selection of brides and marriage, working of married women, selection of occupation etc. The study concludes that the students have largely remained and are more likely to remain fully or highly traditional in two central areas concerning joint family and caste endogamy. On the other hand, in the remaining seven areas, which are peripheral, they have largely remained and are more likely to remain partially deviated; seeking adjustments by partially modifying the traditional norms in such a way as to accommodate their new individual aspirations and to suit the new industrial and urban conditions, which they are going to live in. The limitation of the study is that it does not include female youth. However it is mentioned here because of the similarity of certain topics.

Rajendra Pandey (1969) in *'Youth Culture: Nature and Content*

– *some approaches'*[7] provides a mixture of discursive interpretation about youth and youth culture. The main concern of the work clearly indicates that there is an urgent need for a unified approach, which should be all inclusive and give a holistic explanation of youth culture- its nature and content. However it is contended here that youth culture is a subculture which consists of all those elements that are essential to sub-culture, for its emergence and existence. According to A. Cohen, the crucial conditions for the emergence of new cultural forms are the existence of effective interaction with one another of a number of actors with similar problems. A sub-culture owes its existence to the fact that it provides a solution to certain problems of adjustment shared amongst a community of individuals. A set of common understanding, sentiments and common loyalties are the important elements of sub-culture. O'Donnell's empirical findings in his book, *The Rise and Decline of a Sub-Culture,* support Cohen's conception of sub-culture, but at the same time it is suggested that, this definition can't claim to be holistic, but it is hoped that it will serve a basis for further analysis and clarification of the concept.

S.C. Dube (1972) in his paper on, *"The Restive Students: Strands and Themes in Contemporary Youth Culture"*, objects to term Indian students or contemporary youth as an 'undifferentiated mass'. In the light of the differences in their background, orientation and outlook, he identifies four sub-cultures of the contemporary youth. These are:

1. The Indian counterpart of the Hippies,
2. The models coming from the Westernized and alienated families,
3. Youths of the medium to low privileged status of society, and
4. The largest group consists of literates and those whose parents have not had the benefits of higher education.

The UNESCO sponsored *'Study of the Youth and Established Culture: Dissent and Cooperation'* by Kirpal Prem in 1976, carried out on Indian youth brings out clearly the widespread frustration of young people and their disillusionment with the functioning of the dominant establishments of culture, especially the political parties and vested interests in the control of several sectors of Indian national society. At the same time, it underlines the healthy frame of mind and outlook of the Indian youth, preferring cooperation to confrontation and projecting values significantly different from the youth of different western countries. In extension, this study throws light on the values and aspiration of the youth and highlights the opportunity for constructive, cooperative and disciplined action by youth for national development. Further the study also reveals the acute need for further research in a field of crucial importance, because the existing data is meager and patchy, and inter-disciplinary projects are needed.

'Rural Youth in Urban India' by P.K. Gandhi in 1983, reveals two different major aspects from the above one. The first aspect relates to the background and consists of analysis of socio-economic background of the rural youth, their educational performance, and motivations for education and attitudes that help or hinder their movement to modernization. The purpose of this part of the study was to know who among the rural areas, were the consumers of higher education and how far their background contributes to creation of youth-culture. In the second part of the study, the focus is on the youth culture, their preferences, leisure, social adjustment and dress etc. The study reveals that youth under reference are exposed to varying degrees of urbanizing forces. However this study for all its intents and purposes may be treated as one of the universe and not a sample.

The study by H.D. Lakshminarayana (1985) entitled *'College Youth: Challenge and Response'* was initiated as part of practical training in research methodology for the post graduate students of sociology in Bangalore University. The main aim of the study was to reveal the responses from the college students on certain issues such as their political perspective, educational and occupational aspirations, cultural orientations and social relations. The study reveals that youth are highly displeased with present education and criticize the system of examination severely for many lapses. But, they are helpless and have compromised with the education they are receiving for whatever worth it is, this is because, college youth have relied more on the decisions of their elders. On the political issues it was rather interesting that youth have no ambition to get the right to franchise at an early age. However, their preferences of political parties indicate that they are not radical as is generally expected in the underdeveloped nations. While job aspirations indicated very limited choice, low caste youth appear to be more hopeful, which may probably be because of policy reservations of jobs for them. Further the study also reveals that our youth, despite modern education' they receive have not fully lost faith in religion and are still entangled in the values of traditional Indian society.

In his study *'Values and Attitudes of Indian Youth'* N.Y. Reddy (1986) investigates the influence of technical, economic and social developments on youth perceptions in macro perspectives and reveals that, what we cherished as permanent values once are no more laudable to the present youth. There is a regular age trend in the development of attitudes in the youth. As the age of the subject increases, there is a tendency towards more and more acquisition of modernization. The study further reveals that subjects coming from rural joint families are more traditionalistic and politically oriented than those coming from urban nuclear families. However, the objective of the study was not to find out the pattern of change in values and attitudes over a period of time, but to know the differences in perceptions of these by youth of different socio-economic backgrounds.

The study *'Youth and Media-Its Implications'*[8] by T.J. Kamalanabhan (1998) was conducted to find out the media habits of youth in relation to their personal and family characteristics. The results of the study reveals that family characteristics of youth like parents education, occupation, income and material standards of living are very much reflected in media possession, media exposure and perception of media autonomy. The personal characteristics of youth such as, type of course and type of school/college also were found to be influenced by their family background, like youth from educated, rich and affluent families have opted for commerce or science rather than arts and had gone to private schools/ colleges rather than Govt. schools/colleges. Besides, the study reveals that male youth have greater media possession and exposure but perceive less credibility and more negative implications as compared to female youth. At the same time the study also indicates that youth from richer families are likely to perceive more positive implications of mass media.

Contemporary Youth in Jammu and Kashmir

Using a broader notion of youth, that includes both adolescents and young adults, the youngers represent the present generation of Jammu and Kashmir youth who are expected to realize the unfulfilled dreams of their parents and who are showered by increasing supplies of commodities as they grow up. They are open to new ideas, yearn for freedom and individuality and either as an individual or in groups, they explore few areas in the public spheres. A noticeable exception was the rapid growth of popular interest in militant and political agitations in 1990's in which, college students in particular and urban youth in general played a key role. Many of the young persons in 18-25 years age group were arrested by the Indian army for getting training in Pakistan and demanding independence.[9] However at present the scenario of youth is different. Their worries, fear and anxiety about their future along with the daily calculated efforts to move themselves ahead take a serious toll on the health of the youth, making many of them physically and mentally fragile. Sometimes in order to overcome the depressions and stress, people mostly youngsters resort to drugs. It is something so evident in the study entitled, *Drug Addiction: A Sociological Study of District Srinagar*, that the majority of respondents i.e., 67 per cent between 21-30 years age group involved in drug addiction were students and unemployed youth.[10] Furthermore, sometimes the outburst of anger, frustration, shame, guilt, and pessimism all breeds suicide. Notwithstanding Jammu and

Kashmir only, according to the, "Accidental Deaths and Suicide in India-2000, National Crime Records Bureau," of the total suicide victims around 35.6 per cent were youth between 15-29 years of age group. Among the specified causes, failure in examinations was the primary cause among youth and adolescents.[11]

Besides this, as in other parts of the country, due to the growing consumerism aggravated by aggressive advertisements there has been a cultural twist also among Jammu and Kashmir youth. They adopted individualistic and fashionable concepts of life and want to go beyond old social norms and create their own new world of norms and habits. There appears to be some linkages between the revival of religious fundamentalism on the one hand and the growing frustration of general public on the other. Increasing social, moral, and psychiatric disorders like growing criminality in the form of robbery, sexual assault and accidental rate in Jammu and Kashmir can possibly be an indicator of the same. For example the study about drug addiction in Srinagar, as mentioned earlier reveals that while ascertaining information about the sources of money for purchase of drugs, 18 per cent respondents said that they purchase drugs out of money earned through illegal means.

The factors that in general appear to have given rise to such issues concerning youth and society at large in last few decades in J&K are the; expansion of education, decreasing employment opportunities, lack of proper guidance, increasing influence of mass media, long hours of training in short term courses such as computers etc. All these and others factors have created a situation in which discrepant choice of cultural norms and artifacts are rendered possible.

Talking about the literature on youth in the context of Jammu and Kashmir; it is rare and is more so in case of Kashmir. However, if any scholarly or media attention on Jammu and Kashmir youth has been focused, that is on young urbanities especially on urban college students of Jammu and Kashmir. The reasons are obvious: urban youth of these regions are more visible to the media, more vocal when being interviewed and easier to be surveyed. More importantly urban youth of Jammu and Kashmir regions spend much more on commodities beyond daily necessities and are more open to fashion trends. In short they are better consumers. But this market driven emphasis on young urban consumers has obscured our understanding of Jammu and Kashmir youth as a whole, because youth in other areas of the state not only constitute a good portion of youth population in Jammu and Kashmir but they too may have essentially the same kind of life aspirations as their counterparts in Jammu and Kashmir regions. Research shows that many of the Ladakhi youth have shown a tendency towards materialism and be much part of the modern world as youth elsewhere in the country. Unlike their parents or older siblings, many want to leave their native places to seek jobs in big cities and be successful, so that they can have materially comfortable life. However, their joys and pains, losses and gains, love and hatred rarely enter the sight of scholars. A report about the contemporary youth in Kashmir narrates certain phenomenon:

A very short essay *Kashmiri Youth Take up Arts amid Conflict* by Nafeesa Syeed, 2011, narrates a story about Uzma Falak who is an accidental artist. After hearing reports of summer 2010 of a boy being gunned down at a playground and a woman killed while adjusting a curtain in a window at her home in Indian-controlled Kashmir, the 21-year-old Falak says she was compelled to pick up a pen. Her blank-verse poem, "The Year of Blood Rain!" came flowing out. "Comrades in teens and twenties/challenged the Rain/Fists held together/high amid the dreadful Rain/Drenched! The comrades moved/Only to share a grave!" reads one stanza.

Falak is among a growing group of Kashmiri youth turning to the arts to express themselves in this restive valley. For some, it's just a personal vent, for others, it's a means of resistance against what they call an invasive occupation by Indian security forces. They range from dabblers to serious amateurs taking up painting, photography, theater, writing, film, and even hip hop to channel their diverse views.

Here, there is an underlying current of discontent, which can be suddenly electrified. There have been youth uprisings and military crackdowns each summer for the past three years, including 2010 unrest when masses of youth were either in the streets pelting stones or stuck at home for months during curfews and strikes.

Now as the snow melts from mountaintops, already separatists have called for strikes, and local media report authorities arresting youth to curb further revolt. In addition, Amnesty International released a report in March 2011, alleging that the state of Jammu and Kashmir is detaining hundreds of people under the Public Safety Act without charge or prosecution. The Indian government has also appointed three interlocutors who have visited the valley and made recommendations on how to handle the situation. This context, locals say, can be the caldron for chaos as well as creativity. "You never know when it starts getting registered in your brain and it comes out in a subconscious way like this," Falak says of the conflict triggering innovation.

Spheres of Expression

At the exclusive lakeside convention center in Srinagar, Kashmir's capital, framed paintings and photographs are mounted onto easels and walls. Poems, some handwritten, are posted on boards. One painting shows a soaring dove trailed by an endless chain. In a photograph, village women walk with metal waterpots atop their heads. There are multiple images of Kashmir's natural beauty. It's all the work of young Kashmiris as part of an exhibit during, a youth-led summit. In addition to the display, hundreds of youngsters spent days listening to experts and tackling issues such as culture, rights, and the economy in small-group discussions during the event, which organizers claim was the "first of its kind."

Conference attendees—teens and 20-somethings dressed in jeans or salwar kameez—line up before a courtyard door, as a handful at a time are allowed outside where scrolls of white banners are unfurled on the pavement and surrounding walls. They shake aerosol cans filled with red, black, and yellow paint and try their hand at graffiti, spray-painting messages such as "Give Peace a Chance" and "Let's Build Kashmir Better" and "Save Kashmir."

According to Mercy Corps, the international development agency that mentored the youth organizing the conference, some 66 per cent of the Kashmir valley's population is under 30 years old. (The figure is based on census numbers and the NGO's own research.) For those born since the outbreak of the armed militancy in 1989, they have come of age amid turmoil. "It's a generation that has come to believe that conflict stands in the way of their future prosperity," says Usmaan Ahmad, Mercy Corps' Kashmir director. Ahmad says the "children of conflict" seek out mediums in which they can have a voice. "It's not just cathartic for them," he says. "There's also a desire and a hope that someone will hear what they have to say." But some youth complain of parents who discourage the arts and they say there are few resources, such as training centers, to help them pursue their interests.

Besides the fine arts, many youth are articulating themselves through the written word, whether it's fiction, poetry, or narrative nonfiction. Yusra Khan and Rifat Mohidin, both 19, attend a weekly creative writing workshop to hone their craft. The women, petite and clad in headscarves, speak assertively as they describe their aims of chronicling Kashmiri voices in their prose. Khan says when she writes, there's no one to clamp down on her thoughts. "If you're living in a conflict zone…you can't express your views like any other place," she says. "It's only writing through which we can express our views."

Some youth are afraid of repercussions for speaking out, but Mohidin says she expresses her opinions freely in her writing, even though elders have warned her about pushing the envelope too far. The use of creative expression is also more constructive than other methods of airing frustration, she said. "Stone-pelting will not help; violence will never help," she says. "I think we should be pre-planned. We should think of ways that will not harm us and will give us some output."

Beyond the Conflict

Although political themes figure prominently in several artists' work, some also say they want to highlight other aspects of life in the valley. Adnan Qureshi, 23, says he likes to capture the "tiny little things" one misses in daily life through his photography. Nature is his chief subject, in an attempt, he says, to show that Kashmir remains a captivating place. In one of his landscapes, a fiery sunset is juxtaposed with the darkened mountain below. A ray of light reaches for the peak—that, he says, represents the "gradient of hope," which is also the title of the piece. Some youth complain of parents who discourage the arts and they say there are few resources, such as training centres, to help them pursue their interests.

As artists here evolve, the 23-year-old says he hopes they can look both backward and forward—tapping into their culture's long tradition of handicrafts, music and the performing arts, as well as conveying narratives aside from the conflict. "When you move beyond the conflict, then your voice becomes unique," says Sajad, who's working on a graphic novel about Kashmir. "You can incorporate your community, your culture, your tradition, your history…and that voice will stand out of thousands of voices around you."

Breaking Convention

As the situation in Kashmir remains unresolved and unpredictable, youth say they will continue to search far and wide for creative outlets. Illahi, 20, has adopted the swagger and swearing of the rappers he grew up admiring—from Eminem and Tupac Shakur to Immortal Technique. He's even got the getup down, with his hoodies and baggy jeans sagging from his thin frame. He says his rhymes have gradually become more political since he began rapping four years ago. Videos of his songs on YouTube and the playlist on his website are popular with youth. "I want to be a voice for Kashmir," Illahi says in his surprisingly low, raspy voice. "You're representing something, you're representing your people." lllahi shrugs at the suggestion that he's a pioneer and shakes off criticism that he's embraced an alien art form. "It's all about expressing yourself and hip hop, is like, you're not afraid," he says. "I'm not afraid of anybody. I can say whatever I want to say."

Therefore, to fill this gap in literature on the youth in India and Jammu and Kashmir and more importantly youth in the valley of Kashmir and in view of the demands and interest for the last two decades from international organization like, United Nations Commonwealth Secretariat and from National Governments, for the production of literature on youth, including rural/tribal and youth of remotest areas; the present study has significant relevance. And is first of its kind in Kashmir in which our effort is to study and understand the change among youth in spheres of education, occupation, and attitude and interests etc.

Notes

1. Januaz, K., S.N. Eisenstadt, Boubakar Ly and Lotika, S., 1988 (eds.) *"Perspectives on contemporary youth,"* United Nations University. pp. 1-4
2. Johan Forans and Goran Bolin. (eds.) 1995. *Youth Culture in Late Modernity,* Sage Publications London. pp. 5-6.
3. UNESCO, 1979, *Youth Mobilization for development in an Asian setting,* UNESCO, Paris. pp. 11-13.
4. General Assembly Resolution 35/36, 34/151, cited from United Nations Publication, New York, 1986, *The situation of Youth in the 1980's and prospects and challenges for the year 2000,* p. 12.
5. *Ibid.,* pp. 12-13.
6. B. Bradford Brown, Reed W. Larson, and T.S. Saraswathi, 2002 (eds.) *The world youth: Adolescence in eight regions of the globe,* p. 384.
7. *Interdiscipline,* Autum 1969, No. 6, pp. 224-237.
8. Journal of Social Science: *Interdisciplinary Reflections of Contemporary Society,* Vol. 2, No. 1, pp. 281-287.
9. Ram Ahuja, 1997, *Op. cit.,* p. 202.
10. M. Amin Bhat and Shazia, 'Drug Addiction - A sociological study of District Srinagar', cit., in *'Reflections: A Compilation of Research Studies, 2002',* J&K State Resource Centre University of Kashmir, pp. 173-185.
11. Anupriyo Mallick, 'Suicide and Youth: A Case Study of Kolkata', *Social Welfare,* July 2007, Vol. 54, No. 4, pp. 28-29.

3
Locating Youth in Kashmir

Theoretical Models/Perspectives on Social Problems

Every science, including sociology, accumulates knowledge through interplay between theory and research. A theory is a set of statements that explains the relationship between phenomena. The key role of theories is to tell us why something occurred. They help us organize the data from research into a meaningful whole.[1]

As theory provides a point of view for the study of specific problems, an attempt is made here to introduce some of the relevant theories with the ultimate aim of applying them in the empirical data analysis and discussion.[2] Major theories covered are:

1. Structural Functional Theory;
2. Conflict Theory;
3. Exchange and Reference Group Theory;
4. Production Relations.

1. Structural Functional Theory

Structural functionalism has its family tree in the work of early sociologists, especially Emile Durkheim and Max Weber. Among modern-day scholars, it is most closely associated with the work of Talcot Parsons and Robert Merton.

The term "structure" and "function" refers to two separate but closely related concepts. Structure can be compared to the organs or parts of the body of an animal, and functions can be compared with the purposes of these structures. Like a biological structure, a social system is composed of many interrelated and interdependent parts or structures with specific functions. Central to an understanding of social structures is the concepts of "status" and "role". Simply defined, a status is a socially defined position. Status is both ascribed and achieved.

Each social system performs certain functions that make it doable for society and the people who comprise that society to exist. Each serves a purpose that leads to the continuation or firmness of the larger society. The functionalist perspective assumes that these social systems have an underlying tendency to be in symmetry or balance; and system that fails to fulfill its functions will result in an imbalance or disequilibrium. In acute cases, the entire system can breakdown when a change or failure in any one part of the system frequently provokes changes elsewhere in the system.[3]

According to Merton, a social system can have both manifest functions and latent functions. Manifest functions are intentional and recognized; latent functions are neither intentional nor recognized. Merton recognized that not consequences of systems are functional-that is, they do not lead to the maintenance of the system. Some lead to unsteadiness or the collapse of a system. These consequences he termed dysfunctions. Robert Merton's theory of functional alternatives provides one way to avoid such dysfunctions. Functional alternatives are other ways to achieve the intentional goal.

2. *Conflict Theory and its Application*

The conflict perspective in modern sociology derives its brainwave from the work of Karl Marx who saw the struggle between social classes as the 'engine' of history and the main source of social change. Among its latest proponents are such people as Mills, Lewis Coser (1956) and Dahrendorf. They share the view that society is best understood and analyzed in terms of conflict.

Karl Marx began with a very simple assumption: the structure of society is determined by economic organization, predominantly the ownership of property. Inherent in any economic system that supports inequality are forces that generate revolutionary class conflict.

The browbeaten classes sooner or later recognize their submissive and inferior status and revolt against the dominant class of property owners and employers. In conflict theory, it is assumed that societies are in a continuous state of change, in which conflict is a permanent trait, "conflict" does not necessarily imply utter violence; it includes tension, competition and disagreement over goals and values.

Conflict theory tells us to look for the hidden strains and frustrations, mainly between those in power who make the verdict by those involved does not mean the absence of conflict. Conflicting relationships is neither always explicit nor always expressed by individuals. The employees might not openly express their discontent because they may feel that they are powerless to change the situation. In fact, many sociologists have suggested that people fail to express dissatisfaction not because they feel powerless to change things, but they may not be aware that things could be better than what it is, or because they are resigned to the situation. However, there are some clues that could help one to recognize conflict.

Like structural functionalism, conflict theory is used by sociologists to: (1) Explain the relationship between the parts of a social system and the inequalities that exist between these parts; (2) Discover and explain the sources of the conflict; and (3) Help create techniques to deal with conflict.

3. Production Relations

The social relations which men enter into the course of producing material wealth of a society as its fundamental, both in determining the structure of society and its development. The relations of production are the relations not between the human produce and nature, but between the human beings themselves as they occupy different places in society as a result of the division of labour, which is the basic character of human population.

According to Marx the relations of production form the

economic structure of society. And this economic structure is the base not only for the other aspects of economic life, such as distribution and consumption, but also for the whole of the society with its other structures. Marx even identified the relations of the production with the relations of property as their legal expression.[4]

In Marxist theory, the mode of production can be defined as the labour process-forces of production, the relationship between the workers and the owners of the means of production, and between the workers and the product. Secondly, the mode of production is itself reproduced through the interactive process of economic, ideological and political mechanisms intrinsic to itself, and through its subordination of or by other modes of production. Thirdly, the mode of production embodies contradictions at each of these points which both drive it forward and develop the conditions for its own disintegration through the development of class struggle and of class alliance involving those enmeshed in the surrounding modes of production.[5]

Relations of exploitation or, to be more precise, the relations of surplus appropriation, are central to relations of production. This is the relation through which the immediate producers are alienated from the control of surplus of their labour.[6]

4. Exchange and Reference Group Theory

Exchange Theory is generally acknowledged to have been formulated by George Homans and developed by Peter Blau, with subsequent refinements by Richar Emerson and others.[7] This perspective is based on the belief that life is a series of exchanges involving rewards and costs. In economic exchanges, people exchange money, goods, and services, hoping to profit or at least break even in the exchange. Exchange theory assumes that people seek rewarding statuses, relationship, and experiences and try to avoid costs, pain and punishments. Given a set of alternatives, individuals choose those from which they expect the most profit, rewards, or satisfaction and avoid those that are not profitable, rewarding, or satisfying. When the costs exceed the rewards, people are likely to feel angry and dissatisfied. When the rewards exceed the costs, they are likely to feel that they got a good deal. Both parties are more likely to be satisfied with the interaction if there is perceived equity in the exchange, a feeling on the part of both the rewards were worth the costs.

There are two different schools of thought in the exchange theory perspective. George Homans believed that behaviour could be explained in terms of rewards and punishments. In exchange theory, the rewards and punishments are the behaviour of other people, and thus involved in exchanges assume that their rewards will be proportional to their costs. Peter Blau is the advocate of a different school of exchange theory. Blau argued that the exchange is more subjective and interpretative and that the exchanges occur on the symbolic level. As a result, money may be a just reward only if it is defined by the receiver as such, and psychic rewards of satisfaction with doing a good job or of pleasing someone may be as important as money, gifts, or outward responses of praise. Both agreed that all exchange involves a mutually held expectation that reciprocation will occur. If resources or exchange criteria are unequal, one person is at a distant disadvantage and the other has the control and power over the relationship. If there is indeed an imbalance of rewards and costs to one or all of the parties, then there must be some form of negotiation to restore the necessary balance of exchange.

Organizations engaged in exchanges are governed by their relative resources and by the norms of reciprocity and fairness. The society as a whole becomes stratified by the same kind of differentiation that characterizes its individuals. Overall solidarity is generated by "generalized media" of exchange: norms or laws, which codify the principles of exchange into abstract principles. Individuals learn these norms when socialized into society's system of common values. Possessions of these norms then make it possible for exchanges to take place at a distance, instead of through direct interaction.[8]

Reference Groups according to George Herbert Mead and Robert Merton serve two kinds of functions: (1) Set standard for the behaviours of the individual. The individual takes the standards and value judgments of the reference groups and shapes his/her attitudes and behaviour in accordance with them. Such reference groups are called as "normative" reference group, and (2) provides a frame of comparison relative to which the individual evaluate himself/herself and others. They provide a context for evaluating the relative position of the individual and others. Such groups are known as "comparative" reference groups.

Using the Theoretical Perspectives

The major elements of each perspective and its view on social problems have been outlined in the Table 3.1. The perspectives should be seen as three different "tools", each of which is useful in analyzing particular social problems.[9]

Constructing Social Problems

Use of the theoretical perspectives can be illustrated by looking at an important element of the study of social problems: how a social condition becomes a social problem. The existence of a condition alone, even when the condition produces negative consequences, does not make it a social problem; to become a social problem, it must be so defined by some group (Best, 1994; Holstein and Miller, 1993; Spector and Kitsuse, 1987). This process of social definition or construction involves a number of elements: how and why groups identify conditions as problems, how the groups develop an understanding of the causes of the problems, and how situations are developed and implemented. Each of the three perspectives contributes to our understanding of this process.[10]

From the *functionalist perspective*, the social construction of social problems depends, at least in part, on the extent of social disruption or social disorganization produced by a social condition. Conditions that are more disruptive are more likely to be defined as social problems by significant groups or large numbers of people. But many social conditions disrupt the lives of only some people, and these conditions may be defined as problems by some groups but not others.

Table 3.1: An Outline of the Sociological Perspectives

	Functionalism	*Conflict Theory*	*Interactionism*
View of Society	A system of interrelated and interdependent parts	Made up of groups struggling with one another over scarce resources	Individuals in face to face interaction create social consensus
View of the Individual	People are shaped by society to perform important functions for society	People are shaped by the position of their groups in society	People are symbol manipulators who create their social world through social interaction and consensus
View of Social Change	The social system tends to resist change as disruptive	Change is inevitable and continuous	Change occurs when there is no shared consensus about expected behaviour and newly found consensus develops
View of Social Problems	Caused by dysfunctional activities or disorganization in the social system	Arise when group believes its interests are not being served and works to overcome perceived disadvantage	Arise when a condition is defined as stigmatizing or disruptive of normal social expectations
Key Concepts	Integration, interdependence, stability, equilibrium	Interest, power, dominance, conflict, coercion	Interpretation, consensus, shared expectations, specially created reality

The *conflict perspective* helps us recognize that elites and others with access to resources or power play a greater role in this process of social definition: it is the condition that negatively affect their values and way of life that are most likely to be defined as social problems. So, definitions of social problems are constructed out of the clash of competing interest groups.

The *interactionist perspective* recognize the importance of symbols and social meanings in shaping human life, and it points out that defining a "condition" as a "problem" is a matter of attaching certain negative meanings to the condition. The process of interpretation is central to human social life, and people have to interpret a set of objective conditions as something that is 'bad' or 'negative' before they will act on it.

This brief illustration of constructing social problems demonstrates how using the three perspectives can provide a more complete understanding of a topic. This social construction process is complex and continuous, and the resulting social definitions are constantly shifting and changing.

Youth in Kashmir

Each of sociology's major theoretical paradigms addresses the significance of youth in social organization. Sociologists have explored questions of youth and youth issues from several theoretical perspectives, including structural functionalism and conflict theory. After going through the extensive scanning of literature and the empirical evidence from the field in the valley of Kashmir the structural functional and conflict perspective fits into the understanding and application of youth and the issues of youth in Kashmir. The literature which has been generated on youth and youth issues in different sectors around world and India in particular suggest the relevance of major theoretical approaches. Since youth in Kashmir is unique and different in its socio-economic profile and dimensions because of violence and conflict from last twenty five years, the relevance of a particular theory to the application of the phenomenon/problem is extremely significant and the whole discourse is to be seen through the prism of that perspective.

The structure of the society in Kashmir has been structured by the political elite both main stream and separatist groups in such a way that the interests of the state and sub-state as well as separatists structures are well served. Understanding these processes and structural adjustments is the primary task to actually find a relevance of the theoretical frame and various models of youth and youth problems but the matter is complex. Historically these problems were understood within the confines of the Marxist-Leninist principles with their classical approach to almost all social phenomena. According to Marx the relations of production form the economic structure of society. And this economic structure is the base not only for the other aspects of economic life, such as distribution and consumption, but also for the whole of the society with its other structures. According to Karl Marx result of buying children and young persons of underage by the capitalist is physical deterioration and moral degradation. And the perspective fits in well where state is a capitalistic agency which structures the labour of even young and adults for meeting its capitalistic interests and goals.

The conflict perspective is equally relevant to the structural and functional base of youth and youth issues in Kashmir. The public resentment is very high against the operational system of the state and separatist parties but is hidden due to the repressive character of the state and its machinery. The whole discourse finds strong public resentment but those who try to challenge could face punishments and large numbers of people against this system are imprisoned and languishing in jails. So it becomes clear that there is a strong conflict of interests between the public agencies and the agencies of state. But since state is always very powerful especially under such a structure where even very less number of people participate in elections and other political episodes of state, so the public resentment against the system is heavy but hidden. In that perspective the conflict theoretical frame is quite relevant and applicable to the understanding of youth and youth related issues.

Notes

1. Thomus, J. Sullivan, 2000. *Introduction to Social Problems.* Fifth Edition: Allyn and Bacon. p. 9.
2. P. Anandarajakumar, 2004. *Female Child Labour in India.* New Delhi. APH Publishing House. pp. 20-26.
3. *Ibid.,* pp. 20-26.
4. Weilenga, Bastiaan, 1991. *Introduction to Marxism.* Bangalore: Centre for Social Action. pp. 26-27.

5. H.C. Srivastava and Chaturvedi, M.K., 1986. *Rural Middlemen-Network of Patronage.* New Delhi: Ashish Publishing House. p. 113.
6. Venkatesh B. Athreya, *et. al.* 1990. *Barriers Broken—Production Relations and Agrarian Change in Tamil Nadu.* New Delhi: Sage Publications. p. 13.
7. Randall Collins. 1997. *Theoretical Sociology.* India: Rawat Publications. pp. 338-348.
8. *Ibid.*, pp. 338-348.
9. Thomus J. Sullivan. 2000. *Introduction to Social Problems.* Fifth Edition: Allyn and Bacon. pp. 15-16.
10. *Ibid.*

4
Analytical Perspective

Youth as an important age category has been recognized throughout the world and history. The definitions of youth and the concepts people have of the stages in the life of an individual differ from time to time, region to region and culture to culture. There is considerable variation in the use of the term *youth* throughout history. For Aristotle and for all antiquity, there were only three ages of human beings: childhood, youth and old age. In Aristotle's usage *youth* is any age from about 7 to 40 or even 45 years. Similarly Rousseau, the French scholar is said to have used the term *youth* for 'young person'. There is no unanimity on the operational definition of youth as an age category. According to the United Nations, the term *youth* is used to indicate young men and women between the age group of 14-25 years. In the Indian context those belonging to the 15-35 age group, are categorized as youth. According to the encyclopaedia of social work in India the youth belong to the age group of 16-24.

Relevance and Significance

Research on youth living in the margins of the local, the national and the global, became a growth industry among social scientists working in wide ranging settings. Unfortunately in this growing field, very less focus has been paid on contemporary youth who have come up age in a remarkably complicated and tension filled place like Kashmir, where youth have witnessed great changes, and are struggling with uneven local entanglements in national and global projects and processes. There has not been any considerable attempt by social scientists to empirically identify the different aspects, conditions and problems concerning Kashmiri youth with special reference to their educational and occupational aspirations, their values and attitudes, culture and sub-culture etc.

However, this lack of research in Kashmir has obscured our understanding of the Jammu and Kashmir youth as a whole. Youth in Kashmir not only constitute an important portion of youth population in India, but also have essentially the same kind of life aspirations as their counterparts in other regions of the country beyond the impact of conflict and violence from the last more than two decades. The data generated from the study in relation to youth in Kashmir provide the basis for arriving at the firm conclusions based on the following objectives.

Objectives

The objectives of the Youth Study were to identify key transitions experienced by youth, including those pertaining to education, work force participation, sexual activity, marriage, health and civic participation; decision-making and attitudes; leisure and sports; and, to identify key factors underlying young people's sexual and reproductive health knowledge, attitudes and life choices.

- To find out the socio-economic characteristics of the youth and to understand certain attitudes, aspirations and value orientations of the youth in Kashmir.
- To know the youth's access and equity in education, and valuation for education and their particular implications for youth.
- To examine the perceptions and attitudes of the youth regarding the experiences in violent conflict situations in Jammu and Kashmir and the possible role of the youth to improve collective understanding and capacity to work for peace and development in Jammu and Kashmir.

- To assess the extent, magnitude and factors of unemployment and under-employment and to know the social and political implications of the prolonged unemployment and economic exclusion.
- To know the nature and direction of change among youth in Kashmir under the influence of modernization, mass media, industrialization etc. in the areas of education and occupation, social control, state of individualism verses collectivism, leisure patterns and entertainment orientation.

Short Methodology

The statistical data and other empirical material generated and utilized are based on both primary and secondary sources. A sample of 1000 respondents (comprising of 800 youth, 50 government officials, 50 local scholars/intellectuals, 50 social notables/workers and 50 knowledgeable senior citizens) were selected to give representation to all areas, gender, ethnicity, rural, semi-rural, urban, semi-urban and income-occupational-educational groups and sub-groups while a detailed predetermined and structured interview schedule was used for youth selected through stratified random sampling and conducted by professional staff whose services were hired on the basis of having proficiency in Urdu, English and local Kashmiri language. A pilot survey of 100 respondents was conducted before administering the actual study. The proposed sample was distributed for proportional representation into each stratum. In-depth interviews with social notables, senior citizens, knowledgeable persons, men and Government officers were carried out within the limits of interview guide. Special focus was made on the conflict ridden sections and marginalized communities. The secondary data is comprised of the information collected from books, journals, reports, newspapers, periodicals, internet, published and unpublished documents/thesis. An attempt has also been made to introduce some of the relevant theories like functionalist perspective, socio-political conflict and theories of youth with the ultimate aim to apply them in the empirical data analysis and discussion.

Amidst the plethora of literature being generated on youth at the global level, the present work on the same subject will be distinguished by its extensiveness and holistic treatment. Not only that a considerable number of youth representing every stratum of the society were interviewed but their parents and colleagues, friends, groups etc. were also taken care off to make the study multidimensional in character. The ethnographic accounts and case studies surely helped to provide a holistic picture of the youth and youth issues.

Rationale

For the operational definition of the concept of youth it is agreed that despite of its fluidness and arbitrarily defined, 10-35 years of life is an eventful time, a period in which young people in most of the cultures experience changes in their roles and shifts in social expectations of them. While today's youth are healthier, more urbanized and better educated than earlier generations, social vulnerabilities persist and transitions to adulthood are too frequently marked by early entry into the labour force, abrupt and premature exit from schools and colleges, and strongly-held gender norms. In the course of the transition to adulthood, moreover, young people face significant risks related to sexual and reproductive health. In recognition of the importance of investing in young people, several national policies formulated since 2000, including the National Population Policy 2000 (MOHFW, 2000) and the National Youth Policy 2003 (Ministry of Youth Affairs and Sports, 2003) have underscored a commitment to addressing the multiple needs of this group in India. Effective implementation of both policies and programmes, however, has been handicapped by the lack of evidence on young people's situation and needs. Currently available evidence is limited, at best, and comes largely from small-scale and unrepresentative studies. The information that is available on young people's various transitions remains limited and the small sample sizes obtained preclude the possibility of in-depth analysis and of obtaining representative estimates of behaviours and practices among different sub-groups of young people.

Locale

A brief overview of the demographic, socio-economic and reproductive health situation in the country as a whole and Jammu and Kashmir in particular in which the Youth Study was undertaken suggests that while distributions of the population in Jammu and Kashmir were similar to that of the national population, there is considerable diversity across different states in India. India's population, which crossed one billion in 2000, reached 1.2 billion in 2011; it is one of the youngest countries in the world, with almost one-third (31%) of its population aged 10–24 and almost one-fifth (18%) aged 15–24 (Office of the Registrar General and Census Commissioner, 2001a). The current age structure implies a low dependency ratio, an advantage characterized as the demographic dividend. As far as the sex ratio is concerned, India's population continues to be characterized by population and child sex ratios that are unfavourable to females: the population sex ratio stood at 940 females per 1,000 males in 2011. The distribution of the population by religion indicates that 81 per cent of the national population was Hindu, 13 per cent was Muslim and the remaining 6 per cent belonged to other religions, including Buddhists, Christians, Jains and Sikhs in 2001. As far as the urban population is concerned, the vast majority of India's population lives in rural areas, 72 per cent; population density was 325 per square kilometer for the country as a whole in 2001. The country has witnessed considerable intra- and inter-state migration during the decade 1991–2001; during this period, a total of 98 million persons migrated within or outside the state of last residence.

Although economic growth has decelerated in India with the global financial meltdown and consequent economic recession, India currently is the second fastest growing economy in the world (Ministry of Finance, 2009a). Despite the impressive performance of the Indian economy, poverty remains a major concern. As of 2004–05, over one-quarter (27.5%) of the country's population was living below the poverty line, with little difference between those residing in urban (25.7%) and rural (28.3%) areas (Planning Commission,

2007b). Although government expenditure in the educational sector has gone up consistently over the years, a significant proportion of the population remains illiterate, with wide geographic and gender disparities. For example, the overall literacy rate in the country was just 65-75 per cent among males and 54 per cent among females—in 2001.

Jammu & Kashmir is India's northern-most state, lying between six mountain ranges and covering an area of 2,22,236 sq. kilometers. It is located between 32°17′ and 36°58′ North latitude, and between 37°26′ and 80°30′ East longitude. The state commonly known as Kashmir is bounded on the north by Afghanistan and China, on the east by China, on the south by the state of Himachal Pradesh and the state of Punjab in India, and on the west by the North-West Frontier Province and the Punjab Province of Pakistan. Jammu and Kashmir actually comprises of three regions: the foothill plains of Jammu; the lakes and blue valleys of Kashmir rising to alpine passes, the high altitude plains and starkly beautiful mountains of Ladakh which lies beyond narrow passes.

History

Hari Singh had ascended the throne of Kashmir in 1925 and was the reigning monarch at the conclusion of British rule in the subcontinent in 1947. One of the conditions of the partition of India imposed by Britain was that the rulers of princely states would have the right to opt for either Pakistan or India or remain independent. In 1947, Kashmir's population was 77 per cent Muslim and it shared a boundary with both Dominion of Pakistan and Union of India. On 20 October 1947, tribesmen backed by Pakistan invaded Kashmir. The Maharaja initially fought back but appealed for assistance to the Governor General Louis Mountbatten, who agreed on the condition that the ruler accedes to India. Hari Singh signed the Instrument of Accession on 26 October 1947 and it was accepted on 27 October 1947 by the Governor General of India. Once the Instrument of Accession was signed, Indian soldiers entered Kashmir with orders to evict the raiders, but they were not able to expel everyone from the state by the time the harsh winter started.

India took the matter to the United Nations. The UN resolution asked both India and Pakistan to vacate the areas they had occupied and hold a referendum under UN observation. The holding of this plebiscite, which India initially supported, was dismissed by India because the 1952 elected Constituent Assembly of Jammu and Kashmir voted in favour of confirming the Kashmir region's accession to India. Another reason for the abandonment of the referendum is because demographic changes after 1947 have been effected in Pakistan administered Kashmir, as generations of Pakistani individuals' non-native to the region have been allowed to take residence in Pakistan-administered Kashmir. Furthermore, in Jammu & Kashmir state of India, the demographics of the Kashmir Valley have also been altered after separatist militants coerced 250,000 Kashmiri Hindus to leave the region. Moreover, Pakistan failed to withdraw its troops from the Kashmir region as was required under the same UN resolution of 13 August 1948 which discussed the plebiscite.

Diplomatic relations between India and Pakistan soured for many other reasons, and eventually resulted in three further wars in Kashmir – the Indo-Pakistani War of 1965, the Indo-Pakistani War of 1971 and the Kargil War in 1999. India has control of 60 per cent of the area of the former Princely State of Jammu and Kashmir (Jammu, Kashmir Valley, and Ladakh); Pakistan controls 30 per cent of the region (Gilgit-Baltistan and Azad Kashmir). China occupied 10 per cent (Aksai Chin) of the state in 1962. The eastern region of the erstwhile princely state of Kashmir has also been beset with a boundary dispute. In the late 19th and early 20th centuries, although some boundary agreements were signed between Great Britain, Tibet, Afghanistan and Russia over the northern borders of Kashmir, China never accepted these agreements, and the official Chinese position did not change with the Communist Revolution in 1949. By the mid-1950s the Chinese army had entered the northeast portion of Ladakh. By 1956–57 they had completed a military road through the Aksai Chin area to provide better communication between Xinjiag and western Tibet. India's belated discovery of this road led to border clashes between the two countries that culminated in the Sino-Indian war of October 1962. China has occupied Aksai Chin since 1962 and, in addition, an adjoining region, the Trans Karakoram Tract was ceded by Pakistan to China in 1963.

For intermittent periods between 1957, when the state approved its own Constitution, and the death of Sheikh Abdullah in 1982, the state had alternating spells of stability and discontent. In the late 1980s, however, simmering discontent over the high-handed policies of the Union Government and allegations of the rigging of the 1987 assembly elections triggered a violent uprising which was backed by Pakistan, the foreign hand. Since then, the region has seen a prolonged, bloody conflict between militants and the Indian Army, both of whom have been accused of widespread human rights abuses, including abductions, massacres, rapes and lootings. The army has officially denied these allegations. However, militancy in the state has been on the decline since 1996, also again in 2004 with the peace process with India and Pakistan. Furthermore the situation has become increasingly peaceful in recent years.

Geography and Climate

Jammu and Kashmir is home to several valleys such as the Kashmir Valley, Tawi Valley, Chenab Valley, Poonch Valley, Sindh Valley and Lidder Valley. The main Kashmir valley is 100 km (62 miles) wide and 15,520.3 km^2 (5,992.4 sq. miles) in area. The Himalayas divide the Kashmir valley from Ladakh while the Pir Panjal range, which encloses the valley from the west and the south, separates it from the Great Plains of northern India. Along the northeastern flank of the Valley runs the main range of the Himalayas. This densely settled and beautiful valley has an average height of 1,850 meters (6,070 ft.) above sea-level but the surrounding Pir Panjal range has an average elevation of 5,000 meters (16,000 ft.).

Because of Jammu and Kashmir's wide range of elevations, its biogeography is diverse. North western scrub forests and Himalayan tropical pine forests are found in the low elevations of the far southwest. These give way to a broad band of western broad leaf forests running from northwest-southeast across the Kashmir Valley. Around the highest elevations, there is no vegetation, simply rock and ice. The Jhelum River is the only major Himalayan River which flows through the Kashmir valley. The Indus, Tawi, Ravi and Chenab are the major rivers flowing through the state. Jammu and Kashmir is home to several Himalayan glaciers. With an average altitude of 5,753 meters (18,875 ft.) above sea-level, the Siachen Glacier is 70 km (43 miles) long making it the longest Himalayan glacier.

The climate of Jammu and Kashmir varies greatly owing to its rugged topography. In the south around Jammu, the climate is typically monsoonal, though the region is sufficiently far west to average 40 to 50 mm (1.6 to 2 inches) of rain per month between January and March. In the hot season, Jammu city is very hot and can reach up to 40°C (104°F) whilst in July and August, very heavy though erratic rainfall occurs with monthly extremes of up to 650 millimeters (25.5 inches). In September, rainfall declines, and by October conditions are hot but extremely dry, with minimal rainfall and temperatures of around 29°C (84°F). Across from the Pir Panjal range, the South Asian monsoon is no longer a factor and most precipitation falls in the spring from southwest cloud bands. Because of its closeness to the Arabian Sea, Srinagar receives as much as 635 millimeters (25 inch) of rain from this source, with the wettest months being March to May with around 85 millimeters (3.3 inches) per month. Across from the main Himalaya Range, even the southwest cloud bands break up and the climate of Ladakh and Zanskar is extremely dry and cold. Annual precipitation is only around 100 mm (4 inches) per year and humidity is very low. In this region, almost all above 3,000 meters (9,750 ft.) above sea level, winters are extremely cold. In Zanskar, the average January temperature is –20°C (–4°F) with extremes as low as –40°C (–40°F). All the rivers freeze over. Locals make river crossings during this period because their high levels from glacier melt in summer inhibits crossing. In summer in Ladakh and Zanskar, days are typically a warm 20°C (68°F), but with the low humidity and thin air nights can still be cold.

Administrative Divisions

Jammu and Kashmir consists of three divisions: Jammu, Kashmir Valley and Ladakh, and is further divided into 22 districts. The Siachen Glacier, although under Indian military control, does not lie under the administration of the state of Jammu and Kashmir. Kishtawar, Ramban, Reasi, Samba, Bondipora, Ganderbal, Kulgam and Shopian are newly formed districts, and their areas are included with those of the districts from which they were formed.

Demographics

Jammu and Kashmir has a Muslim majority population. Though Islam is practiced by about 67 per cent of the population of the state and by 97 per cent of the population of the Kashmir valley, the state has large communities of Buddhists, Hindus. In Jammu, Hindus constitute 65 per cent of the population, Muslims 31 per cent and Sikhs, 4 per cent; In Ladakh, Buddhists constitute about 46 per cent of the population, the remaining being Muslims. The people of Ladakh are of Indo-Tibetan origin, while the southern area of Jammu includes many communities tracing their ancestry to the nearby Indian states of Haryana and Punjab, as well as the city of Delhi. In totality, the Muslims constitute 67 per cent of the population, the Hindus about 30 per cent, the Buddhists 1 per cent, and the Sikhs 2 per cent of the population. According to political scientist Alexander Evans, approximately 95 per cent of the total population of 160,000–170,000 of Kashmiri Brahmins, also called Kashmiri Pandits, (*i.e.* approximately 150,000 to 160,000) left the Kashmir Valley in 1990 as militancy engulfed the state. According to an estimate by the Central Intelligence Agency, about 300,000 Kashmiri Pandits from the entire state of Jammu and Kashmir have been internally displaced due to the ongoing violence.

In Jammu and Kashmir, the principal spoken languages are Kashmiri, Urdu, Dogri, Pahari, Balti, Ladakhi, Gogri, Shina and Pashto. However, Urdu written in the Persian script is the official language of the state. Many speakers of these languages use English as a second language. The Kashmir Valley is

Population Districtwise — 2001 and 2011 Census

Name (District)	*Headquarters*	*Area (km²)*	*Population 2001 Census*	*Population 2011 Census*
Kathua	Kathua	2,651	550,084	615,711
Jammu	Jammu	3,097	1,343,756	1,526,406
Samba	Samba		245,016	318,611
Udhampur	Udhampur	4,550	475,068	555,357
Reasi	Reasi		268,441	314,714
Rajouri	Rajouri	2,630	483,284	619,266
Poonch	Poonch	1,674	372,613	476,820
Doda	Doda	11,691	320,256	409,576
Ramban	Ramban		180,830	283,313
Kishtwar	Kishtawar		190,843	231,037
Jammu Division	Jammu	*26,293*	*4,430,191*	*5,350,811*
Anantnag	Anantnag	3,984	734,549	1,069,749
Kulgam	Kulgam		437,885	423,181
Pulwama	Pulwama	1,398	441,275	570,060
Shopian	Shopian		211,332	265,960
Budgam	Budgam	1,371	629,309	755,331
Srinagar	Srinagar	2,228	990,548	1,250,173
Ganderbal	Ganderbal		211,899	297,003
Bandipora	Bandipora		316,436	385,099
Baramullah	Baramullah	4,588	853,344	1,015,503
Kupwra	Kupawra	2,379	650,393	875,564
Kashmir Valley Division	Srinagar	*15,948*	*5,476,970*	*6,907,622*
Kargil	Kargil	14,036	119,307	143,388
Leh	Leh	45,110	117,232	147,104
Ladakh Division	Leh	*59,146*	*236,539*	*290,492*
TOTAL		**101,387**	**10,143,700**	**12,548,925**

Population of Major Cities

Name	*Rank*	*Population 2011 Census*	*State Region*
Srinagar	1	1,192,792	Kashmir
Jammu	2	9,51,373	Jammu
Anantnag	3	2,08,505	Kashmir
Udhampur	4	1,82,778	Jammu
Baramullah	5	1,67,986	Kashmir
Kathua	6	1,62,988	Jammu
Sopore	7	66,963	Kashmir
Rajouri	8	41,552	Jammu
Poonch	9	40,987	Jammu
Leh	10	27,513	Ladakh
Bandipora	11	25,714	Kashmir

Population — Major Religion-wise

Division	*Population*	*Muslim*	*Hindu*	*Sikh*	*Buddhist and other*
Kashmir (53.9%)	5,476,970	97.16%	1.84%	0.88%	0.11%
Jammu (43.7%)	4,430,191	30.69%	65.23%	3.57%	0.51%
Ladakh (2.3%)	236,539	47.40%	6.22%	–	45.87%
Jammu & Kashmir	**10,143,700**	**66.97%**	**29.63%**	**2.03%**	**1.36%**

dominated by ethnic Kashmiris, who have largely driven the Azadi campaign. Non-Kashmiri Muslim ethnic groups (Paharis, Sheenas, Gujjars and Bakarwalas), who dominate areas along the Line of Control, have remained indifferent to the separatist campaign. Jammu province region has a 70:30 Hindu-Muslim ratio. Parts of the region were hit by militants, but violence has ebbed there, along with the Valley, after India and Pakistan started a peace process in 2004. Dogras (67%) are the single largest group in the multi-ethnic region of Punjabis, Paharis, Bakerwals and Gujjars. Statehood is demanded in Hindu-dominated districts. Ladakh is the largest region in the state with over two hundred thousand people. Its two districts are Leh (77% Buddhist) and Kargil (80% Muslim population).

Union territory status has been the key demand of Leh Buddhists for many years.

Politics and Government

Jammu and Kashmir is the only state in India which enjoys special autonomy under Article 370 of the Constitution of India, according to which no law enacted by the Parliament of India, except for those in the field of defense, communication and foreign policy, will be extendable in Jammu and Kashmir unless it is ratified by the state legislature of Jammu and Kashmir. Subsequently, jurisdiction of the Supreme Court of India over Jammu and Kashmir has been extended. Jammu and Kashmir is also the only Indian state that has its own official flag and constitution, and Indians from other states cannot purchase land or property in the state. Designed by the then ruling National Conference, the flag of Jammu and Kashmir features a plough on a red background symbolizing labour; it replaced the Maharaja's state flag. The three stripes represent the three distinct administrative divisions of the state, namely Jammu, Valley of Kashmir, and Ladakh. Since 1990, the Armed Forces Special Powers Act, which gives special powers to the Indian security forces, has been enforced in Jammu and Kashmir. The decision to invoke this act was criticized by the Human Rights Watch.

Like all the states of India, Jammu and Kashmir has a multi-party democratic system of governance with a bicameral legislature. At the time of drafting the Constitution of Jammu and Kashmir, 100 seats were earmarked for direct elections from territorial constituencies. Of these, 25 seats were reserved for the areas of Jammu and Kashmir State that came under Pakistani occupation; this was reduced to 24 after the 12th amendment of the Constitution of Jammu and Kashmir: "The territory of the State shall comprise all the territories which on the fifteenth day of August 1947, were under the sovereignty or suzerainty of the Ruler of the State" and Section 48 therein states that, "Notwithstanding anything contained in section 47, until the area of the State under the occupations of Pakistan ceases to so occupied and the people residing in that area elect their representatives: (a) twenty-five seats in the Legislative Assembly shall remain vacant and shall not be taken into account for reckoning the total member-ship of the Assembly; and the said area shall be excluded in delimiting the territorial Constituencies under Section 47".

After a delimitation in 1988, the total number of seats increased to 111, of which 87 were within Indian-administered territory. The Jammu & Kashmir Assembly is the only state in India to have a 6-year term, in contrast to the norm of a 5-year term followed in every other state's Assembly. There was indication from the previous INC Government to bring parity with the other states, but this does not seem to have received the required support to pass into law. Influential political parties include the Jammu and Kashmir National Conference (NC), the Indian National Congress (INC), the Jammu And Kashmir People's Democratic Party (PDP), the Bharatiya Janata Party (BJP) and other smaller regional parties. After dominating Kashmir's politics for years, the National Conference's influence waned in 2002, when INC and PDP formed a political alliance and rose to power. Under the power-sharing agreement, INC leader Ghulam Nabi Azad replaced PDP's Mufti Mohammad Sayeed as the Chief Minister of Jammu and Kashmir in late 2005. However, in 2008, PDP withdrew its support from the government on the issue of temporary diversion of nearly 40 acres (16 hactares) of land to the Shri Amarnath Shrine Board. In the 2008 Kashmir Elections that were held from 17 November to 24 December, the National Conference party and the Congress party together won enough seats in the state assembly to form a ruling alliance. Some Kashmiris, especially those residing in the Kashmir Valley, demand greater autonomy, sovereignty and even independence from India. Due to the economic integration of Jammu and Kashmir with the rest of India, separatist movements across the Kashmir Valley declined. However, following the unrest in 2008, which included more than 500,000 protesters at a rally on 18 August, secessionist movements gained a boost.

Jammu and Kashmir's economy is predominantly

dependent on agriculture and allied activities. The Kashmir valley is also known for its sericulture and cold-water fisheries. Wood from Kashmir is used to make high-quality cricket bats, popularly known as *Kashmir Willow*. Kashmiri saffron is also very famous and brings the state a handsome amount of foreign exchange. Agricultural exports from Jammu and Kashmir include apples, barley, cherries, corn, millet, oranges, rice, peaches, pears, saffron, sorghum, vegetables, and wheat, while manufactured exports include handicrafts, rugs, and shawls. Horticulture plays a vital role in the economic development of the state. With an annual turnover of over Rs. 300 crore, apart from foreign exchange of over Rs. 80 crore, this sector is the next biggest source of income in the state's economy. The region of Kashmir is known for its horticulture industry and is the wealthiest region in the state. Horticultural produce from the state includes apples, apricots, cherries, pears, plums, almonds and walnuts. The Doda district has deposits of high-grade sapphire. Though small, the manufacturing and services sector is growing rapidly, especially in the Jammu division. In recent years, several consumer goods companies have opened manufacturing units in the region. The Associated Chamber of Commerce and Industry of India have identified several industrial sectors which can attract investment in the state, and accordingly, it is working with the union and the state government to set up industrial parks and special economic zones. In the fiscal year 2005–06, exports from the state amounted to Rs. 1,150 crore. However, industrial development in the state faces several major constraints including extreme mountainous landscape and power shortage.

The Government of India has been keen to economically integrate Jammu and Kashmir with the rest of India. The state is one of the largest recipients of grants from New Delhi, totaling US$ 812 million per year. It also has a mere 4 per cent incidence of poverty, one of the lowest in the country. In an attempt to improve the infrastructure in the state, Indian Railways is constructing the ambitious Kashmir Railways project at a cost of more than US$ 2.5 billion. Trains run on the 119 km Baramullah-Qazigund section. The 17.5 km Qazigund-

Banihal section through the 11 km long Pir Panjal Railway Tunnel has been constructed. Udhampur-Katra section has also been constructed. The Katra-Banihal section is under construction. The route crosses major earthquake zones, and is subjected to extreme temperatures of cold and heat, as well as inhospitable terrain, making it an extremely challenging engineering project. It is expected to increase tourism and travel to Kashmir.

Tourism

Before the insurgency intensified in 1989, tourism formed an important part of the Kashmiri economy. The tourism economy in the Kashmir valley was worst hit. However, the holy shrines of Jammu and the Buddhist monasteries of Ladakh continue to remain popular pilgrimage and tourism destinations. Every year, thousands of Hindu pilgrims visit holy shrines of Vaishno Devi and Amarnath, which has had significant impact on the state's economy. It was estimated in 2007 that the Vaishno Devi Yatra contributed Rs. 4.75 billion to the local economy annually a few years ago. The contribution would be much more now as the numbers of visitors have increased considerably. Foreign tourists have been slower to return. The British government still advises against all travel to Jammu and Kashmir with the exception of the cities of Jammu and Srinagar, travel between these two cities on the Jammu-Srinagar highway, and the region of Ladakh. Tourism in the Kashmir valley has rebounded in recent years, and in 2009, the state became one of the top tourist destinations of India. Gulmarg, one of the most popular ski resort destinations in India, is also home to the world's highest green golf. However, the decrease in violence in the state has boosted the state's economy and tourism. It was reported that more than a million tourists visited Kashmir in 2011.

Culture

Ladakh is famous for its unique Indo-Tibetan culture. Chanting in Sanskrit and Tibetan Language forms an integral part of

Ladakh's Buddhist lifestyle. Annual masked dance festivals, weaving and archery are an important part of traditional life in Ladakh. Ladakhi food has much in common with Tibetan food, the most prominent foods being *thukpa,* noodle soup; and *tsampa,* known in Ladakhi as *Ngampe,* roasted barley flour. Typical garb includes gonchas of velvet, elaborately embroidered waistcoats and boots, and gonads or hats. People adorned with gold and silver ornaments and turquoise headgears throng the streets during various Ladakhi festivals. The *Dumhal* is a famous dance in the Kashmir Valley, performed by men of the Wattal region. The women perform the Rouff, another traditional folk dance. Kashmir has been noted for its fine arts for centuries, including poetry and handicrafts. *Shikaras,* traditional small wooden boats, and houseboats are a common feature in various lakes and rivers across the Valley. The Constitution does not allow people from regions other than Jammu and Kashmir to purchase land in the state. As a consequence, houseboats became popular among those who were unable to purchase land in the Valley and has now become an integral part of the Kashmiri lifestyle. *Kahwa,* traditional green tea with spices and almond, is consumed all through the day in the chilly winter climate of Kashmir. Most of the buildings in the Valley and Ladakh are made from softwood and are influenced by Indian, Tibetan, and Islamic architecture. Jammu's Dogra culture and tradition is very similar to that of neighbouring Punjab and Himachal Pradesh. After Dogras, *Gujjars* form the second-largest ethnic group in Jammu. Known for their semi-nomadic lifestyle, Gujjars are also found in large numbers in the Kashmir Valley. Similar to Gujjars, *Gaddis* are primarily herdsmen who hail from the Chamba region in Himachal Pradesh. Gaddis are generally associated with emotive music played on the flute. The *Bakkarwala*s found both in Jammu and the Vale of Kashmir are wholly nomadic pastoral people who move along the Himalayan slopes in search for pastures for their huge flocks of goats and sheep.

Education

In 1970, the state government of Jammu and Kashmir

established its own education board and university. Education in the state is divided into primary, middle, high secondary, college and university level. Jammu and Kashmir follows the 10+2 pattern for education of children. This is handled by Jammu and Kashmir State Board of School Education (abbreviated as JKBOSE). Various private and public schools are recognized by the board to impart education to students. Board examinations are conducted for students in class VIII, X and XII. In addition there are various *Kendriya Vidyalayas* (run by the Government of India) and Indian Army schools that also impart secondary school education. These schools follow the Central Board of Secondary Education pattern. Notable higher education or research institutes in Jammu and Kashmir include Sher-e-Kashmir Institute of Medical Sciences at Soura Srinagar, National Institute of Technology Srinagar, Government College of Engineering and Technology, Institute of Management, Public-Administration and Rural Development, Srinagar, Jammu and the Government Medical College of Jammu. University-level education is provided by University of Jammu, University of Kashmir, Sheri-Kashmir Universities of Agricultural Sciences and Technology Jammu and Kashmir, Shri Mata Vashno Devi University Jammu, Islamic University of Science and Technology, Baba Ghulam Shah Badshah University, and newly established Central Universities of Kashmir and Jammu besides Institution of Technicians and Engineers (Kashmir).

Policy and Programme Environment

The importance of investing in youth has been recognized in India's Constitution. One of the Directive Principles of State Policy, for example, states that it is imperative that "children are given opportunities and facilities to develop in a healthy manner and in conditions of freedom and dignity and that childhood and youth are protected against exploitation and against moral and material abandonment." A large number of policies and programmes exist in India that has relevance for youth. The National Youth Policy, 2003 focuses on the needs of those aged 13–35, but recognizes adolescents (aged 13–19) as a special group requiring a different approach from that appropriate for young adults (aged 20–35). It recognizes, moreover, the need for a multi-dimensional and integrated approach to serving youth needs and contains wide-ranging objectives. For example, it aims to promote qualities of citizenship and adherence to secular principles and values; ensure educational and training opportunities for youth, facilitate their access to health information and services, and develop their leadership in socioeconomic and cultural spheres. Further, it calls for gender justice and a focus on ensuring that the gender gap in education is narrowed, that young women have access to health services, are free from domestic violence and have access to decision-making processes, and that young men are oriented to respect the status and rights of women.

The proposed National Policy on Skill Development calls for establishing a National Skills Development Initiative that aims to empower individuals through improved skills, knowledge and qualifications to gain access to employment in an increasingly competitive global market (Planning Commission, 2009). The policy aims to meet, by 2022, the skilling needs of 500 million individuals. Objectives are to create opportunities for skill acquisition, with special attention to youth, women, and school drop-outs. To achieve these ambitious goals, public private partnerships are envisaged, and outreach is to be expanded through a variety of mechanisms including skill development centers at village and block levels, mobile training and distance learning programmes. At the same time, the coverage of vocations will be expanded and soft skills such as basic numeracy, literacy, rights, team work and confidence building will be folded into skill development curricula.

Study Phases

The Youth Study comprised three phases and included both a survey and qualitative data gathering exercises.

a) Pre-Study Qualitative Phase

As the Youth Study was one of the first of its kind in Kashmir, precedents did not exist for youth terminologies, particularly with reference to sensitive issues (romantic relationships, sexual experience and so on), youth perceptions or youth willingness to share their experiences with study teams. In order to better understand these matters and to inform the design of the study instrument, focus group discussions were conducted with youth, and key informant interviews conducted with teachers, health care providers, and community and youth leaders, in the first phase of the Youth Study. This phase also offered us an opportunity to explore community reactions to the kinds of issues raised by the study. In the course of this pre-survey qualitative phase, we also conducted in-depth interviews with parents of youth to collect parental perspectives on young people's situation and needs. The discussion focused on the life experiences of the child of interest.

b) Survey Phase

A total of one thousand young people were successfully interviewed from different areas of Kashmir. Youth of districts in the valley were interviewed and observed to have cross district perspective and information from youth. Besides unmarried young boys and girls, married youth were also taken care off in the study to have a multivariate perspective.

c) Post-survey Qualitative Phase

In order to better understand experiences of youth and the factors inhibiting and facilitating safe transitions into expected behaviours, in-depth interviews were conducted with consenting youth respondents who reported certain experiences in the course of the interview. These experiences included, notably, having an opposite-sex romantic partner. Among the married, in addition, experiences included exercising choice in spouse selection. At the conclusion of the interview, interviewers sought the consent of respondents for an in-depth interview. Those who consented were then approached by a trained investigator who conducted the interview in the form of an unstructured conversation. A good number of in-depth interviews (case studies) were completed from all the areas.

Study Instruments

a) Interview Guidelines

For the pre-survey qualitative phase, three sets of guidelines were prepared, one each for focus group discussions, key informant interviews and in-depth interviews. These guidelines were appropriately modified for each youth group (married and unmarried young men and women) and parent group (mothers and fathers of married and unmarried young men and women). As mentioned above, specific guidelines were not prepared for the post-survey in-depth interviews with youth reporting selected behaviours; instead, the interviewers were trained to steer the interview to focus on the experience of interest, and obtain information on the circumstances surrounding the experience and the respondent's own perceptions about the experience.

b) Questionnaires

A total of three questionnaires were developed for the study: youth questionnaire; household questionnaire, and interview guide. The development of individual questionnaires was informed by insights obtained in the pre-survey qualitative phase. Once the pre-survey qualitative phase was completed, the data generated were analyzed to identify the kinds of issues that would be explored in the study, ways of presenting sensitive issues, and terminologies to be used that would be comprehensible and acceptable to youth. The research instrument was finalized after extensive pre-testing. Individual questionnaires were employed to interview eligible youth who resided in the selected universe. The strategy of asking a series of non-sensitive questions in the early part of the interview served two purposes: it enabled the interviewer and respondent to build rapport before sensitive questions were posed; it also permitted the investigator to maintain privacy for sensitive questions, as interested bystanders would usually depart while questions in the early sections were being posed. The individual questionnaires collected information on the following topics:

Background Characteristics: Questions were asked regarding the respondent's age, education and schooling, quality of school or college attended, work patterns including housework and paid employment, vocational training, short-term migration and characteristics of parents.

Media exposure: Respondents were asked whether they were exposed to newspapers, television or the internet. They were also asked about their views on the influence of films and television on their own life as well as young people's lives in general. Puberty: In order to assess the age at which puberty was experienced, respondents were asked to report their age at key signs of maturation. Young women, therefore, were questioned about their experiences while young men were asked about the onset of voice changes and growth of body hair.

Parental interaction/relationship: Detailed questions were asked on the extent of parent-child communication on everyday activities as well as sexual and reproductive issues. Questions were also asked to assess the extent to which a respondent had witnessed parental violence or been the victim of violence perpetrated by a parent during the respondent's growing-up years.

Communication, mobility and decision-making: This section collected information on the person with whom youth were most likely to confide matters related to getting a job, growing up, boy-girl relationships and personal problems. Detailed questions were also asked on decision-making and, for all groups except married males, mobility.

Gender and self-efficacy: In order to evaluate the respondent's gender role attitudes and level of self-efficacy, questions were asked to probe opinions about a range of gender-related issues, such as, for example, the importance of boys' vis-à-vis girls' education, housework and freedom of movement.

Awareness of sexual and reproductive matters: This section probed young people's awareness about sexual relations, pregnancy, contraceptive methods, HIV/AIDS and sexually transmitted infection (STI) as well as the legal minimum age at marriage and conditions under which abortion is legally permitted. It also probed young people's sources of information on sexual matters and contraception, the extent to which they had obtained formal sex or family life education, and their experiences and perceptions about this education.

Connectedness and friendship: Questions relating to connectedness and friendship explored respondents' friendship networks among those of the same sex and activities in which they participated with their friends. This was followed in a gradual fashion by questions on interaction with the opposite sex, whether or not the respondent had exchanged a "proposal" of romantic partnership with someone of the opposite sex and whether the respondent had ever met someone of the opposite sex secretly in a number of likely places.

Pre-marital romantic heterosexual relationships: This was a highly sensitive section, conducted only if complete privacy was assured. The section started by probing the pre-marital romantic and sexual experiences of up to five of the respondent's best friends. This technique, known as anonymous third-party reporting (developed by Rossier, 2003), was used to assess the extent to which youth were more likely to report the romantic and sexual relationships of their peers than their own. Respondents were then asked about their own experiences of pre-marital romantic partnerships and, if reported, detailed questions were asked on the nature of such relationships with the first partner and the last or most recent partner (if more than one partner was reported). Questions were designed to gradually probe sensitive behaviours, for example, starting with whether the respondent had ever held hands with a romantic opposite-sex partner, and continuing with questions on hugging, kissing and finally having sex with the partner. We believe this gradual progression of questions was more culturally appropriate than a single question on premarital sex and provided insights into the range of behaviours youth experienced. Questions were also asked about the characteristics of the romantic partner and parental awareness of and reactions to the romantic relationship.

Marriage process: Questions in this section covered marriage planning, dowry, the participation of the respondent in decision-making related to marriage and the respondent's feelings about his or her own marriage. This section was administered, suitably modified, to both married and unmarried respondents.

Health and health seeking: This section collected information on respondents' experience of common health problems, specifically high fever and injury, as well as symptoms of genital infections in the three months preceding the interview. In addition, respondents were asked whether they had sought treatment for these health issues.

Substance use and violence: A series of questions were asked about consumption of tobacco products, alcohol or drugs. In each case, questions were asked about the use and frequency of use of such substances by family members and by the respondents themselves. Additional questions sought respondents' assessments of the frequency with which young people in their neighbourhoods engaged in violence (fights or beatings) and their own participation in such violence.

Programmes and participation: The final section of the questionnaire collected information on programmes available to young people in the village or neighbourhood in which they resided, and the extent to which they participated in such programmes. All respondents were asked about their participation in community activities, opinions about political processes, secular attitudes and participation in recent elections.

Finally, respondents were asked to identify the most important problem facing youth in their village or neighbourhood. Draft tools were extensively reviewed at meetings with the principal investigator and other relevant staff and experts.

Study Design and Sample Size

The Youth Survey was designed to provide estimates for Kashmir as a whole, as well as for urban and rural areas for each of the four categories of respondents, namely married and unmarried young men and women, separately. The study was not designed to provide estimates at district or sub-district levels.

a) Sample Selection

The study treated rural and urban areas as independent sampling domains and, therefore, drew sample areas independently for each of these two domains. In order to avoid potential risks associated with interviewing both women and men from the same area/residence, we decided to conduct interviews in separate areas for female and male respondents. Within each sampling domain, a systematic multi-stage sampling design was adopted. Sample selection procedures differed somewhat in rural and urban areas, as described below. In each area, the households to be interviewed were selected by systematic sampling. The value of the interval (between one selected household and the next) was determined in advance to ensure a self-weighing design. As mentioned earlier, fewer households needed to be selected in order to obtain our sample of unmarried males and married females. Hence, further intervals were computed, using the target sample for unmarried males and married females. Within each selected household, no more than one married and one unmarried respondent was interviewed, resulting in a maximum of two interviews from any household.

b) Sample Weights

In this Youth Study, the sample was weighted at the level of the sampling domain, that is, urban and rural males and females, respectively, that is, a total of four sampling domains. The sample weight was calculated taking into account differential non-response rates as well as design weights for each domain.

Recruitment, Training and Fieldwork

A dozen young men and women underwent interviewer training and all underwent training for mapping and house-listing exercises in the orientation programme designed for the same. On the basis of performance, a total of 6 youth were recruited as field investigators. Training of interviewers was conducted jointly by principal investigator and other technical staff. Training for field investigators for the main study lasted three days. It included lectures and interactive sessions on a range of issues, such as the sexual and reproductive health situation of youth in India in general and Kashmir in particular, an overview of gender issues, ethical issues in research, violence against women, and mental health, as well as detailed explanations of youth issues. Efforts were also made to enable trainees to overcome their inhibitions about discussing political, sexual and reproductive health matters. Trainees were provided opportunities to ask questions via an anonymous drop-box; questions were then answered in the course of training. Trainees were familiarized with each module of the questionnaire, complicated concepts and questions and their underlying rationale. Role-plays and mock interviews were conducted for each module. Towards the end of the training programme, field practice sessions were organized in which trainees were taken to a rural and urban setting and asked to conduct interviews. The training team comprised of principal investigator and others monitored each trainee's progress on a regular basis and selected as interviewers only those trainees who demonstrated a full understanding of the questionnaire as well as the ability to ask questions appropriately and record responses accurately.

Male interviewers interviewed young men and female interviewers interviewed young women. Each team comprised one field editor who was responsible for field editing, back-checks and quality control of interviews; and one supervisor (most of the times principal investigator was acting as supervisor), responsible for the overall management of fieldwork and team-related logistics as well as assisting in field editing and back-checking. Interviewer and supervisor/editor manuals were prepared, translated into the local language and provided to each team member as appropriate. These manuals clarified the meaning and appropriate coding of every question in the questionnaire. Research officer was deputed to oversee fieldwork, and ensure that correct survey procedures were followed and data quality maintained. Principal investigators made continuous visits to monitor and supervise data collection operations. Each team filled quality control sheets regularly, giving the team, research officers and coordinators a quick view of the quality of ongoing fieldwork. These control sheets were designed to provide information on response rates, and track sensitive issue reporting and interviewer performance.

Ethical Considerations

As this was the first such study in Kashmir in which sensitive political, marital, sexual and reproductive experiences of youth were sought, it was unclear how youth respondents and community members would react. At the same time, it was clear that if youth participated in the interview, its content was likely to prompt questions and problems for which support would be requested. A number of ethical issues arose which influenced the design and implementation of the Youth Study.

First, to address our concern that if interviews with young women and men were conducted in the same residence/area, it could lead to teasing, harassment, harm to girls' reputations and even violence, we decided that the study would be undertaken in one setting for young men and in a completely different set for young women. Likewise, we also ensured that two unmarried brothers or sisters, two married brothers or sisters or two sisters- or brothers-in-law would not be interviewed from the same household in case such a practice caused conflict within the family. Hence, in each household, only one individual from any category was selected for interview. In case both a married and an unmarried individual were selected from a particular household, interviews were conducted separately but simultaneously. Second, youth themselves contributed—albeit indirectly—to the development of the questionnaire. In the course of our pre-survey qualitative phase, youth and key informants informed our study teams of various youth behaviours; youth described the ways in which they referred to various sensitive behaviours and, in order to minimize discomfort during questioning, the scenarios and terminologies described by youth themselves were adapted for use in the most sensitive parts of our questionnaire. Third, interviewers underwent extensive training in ethical issues. Emphasis was laid on explaining the content of the questionnaire, the respondent's right to refuse to participate or answer any question, and informed consent. At the same time, we trained interviewers on how to ask sensitive questions—regarding political and sexual experience, domestic violence and forced sex, in particular—in empathetic and non-judgmental ways, and emphasized the importance of offering to refer those in need to appropriate nearby organizations.

Fourth, teams were instructed to apprise senior citizens and community leaders of the study and seek their support for its implementation in the community. This step ensured that community support was forthcoming and enabled team members to build rapport within the community easily. We note that despite the sensitive nature of the questions, not a single area or even the sensitive localities of Kashmir refused permission to Youth Study teams on the grounds of study content, although in Maisuma and some downtown localities of Srinagar, interviews could not be completed with all the selected individuals because of difficult law and order conditions. Fifth, even though consent was sought from each individual to be interviewed, in the case of unmarried youth aged 15–23, consent was also sought from a parent or guardian if the interview was conducted with the family or household. Sixth, all questionnaires were anonymous and names were never recorded. In order to preserve the confidentiality of the respondent or the parent/guardian, signing the consent form was optional; however, the interviewer was required to sign that she or he had explained the content of the consent form to the respondent or parent. Consent forms were detached and stored separately from the questionnaires. Seventh, every effort was made to maintain privacy in the course of the interview. Interviewers were permitted to skip to relatively non-sensitive sections in case the interview was observed by parents or other family members. If possible, particularly in the case of young men, interviews were held outside the home—often in a nearby field or where the youth were available—in order to ensure privacy. Each team was trained to assign one interviewer to conduct parallel discussion sessions with bystanders, thereby providing privacy to the interview. This proved particularly useful in the case of interviews with young women. Finally, interviewers were instructed that if privacy could not be ensured, the interview must be terminated without asking sensitive questions. Due to these strategies, few interviews had to be terminated for want of privacy and in no case were a young respondent's privacy breached.

Eighth, the study team realized that this was perhaps one of the first opportunities many youth would have to discuss intimate matters and that respondents might request information on political, sexual and reproductive issues or seek counseling or treatment for a health problem. In each area/ locality, therefore, the team approached various groups/ organizations that conduct youth- or health-related activities at the city/district level and sought their consent for referring any youth in need to their organization. Many agreed, and youth (and some adults) in need were later referred to these organizations, along with an indication that the individual had been part of the Youth Study. At the same time, research officers and team members themselves built rapport with public health authorities and referred to their facilities those who preferred to seek public services, again, along with the information that the individual had been part of the Youth Study. Finally, many youth were in need of information on political, sexual and reproductive health matters. On occasion, interviewers themselves responded to their questions.

Data Processing

All completed questionnaires were collected for editing and data processing. Completed questionnaires were rechecked and further edited for omissions and consistency. Responses to open-ended questions were scrutinized and common responses were interpreted in codes. For entering the edited data, word and excel software packages were used. Data were entered twice to minimize entry problems. The raw data were validated and cleaned to remove possible inconsistencies. The analysis of data was carried out using word and excel.

5
Youth and Life Course in Kashmir

The idea of embedding the experiences of youth within the life cycle is a positivistic approach in which the individuals' journey through life is presented as normative and de-contextualized. In other words, key sets of experiences are closely linked to age-related stages in a developmental process. Life cycle is essentially linear with one set of age-related experiences (such as leaving school) being closely related to another (gaining full-time employment or getting married). It is well proved that youth have very special role in any country's development. India has the largest youth population and it is well recognized that the youth power is very essential in the development of India and to make India a better place to live. Today if we look upon the condition of the country it is still in developing mode. Former president Dr. A.P.J. Abdul Kalam said that India will be in the list of developed countries by 2020 but by seeing the present scenario it doesn't seem to be possible. India is not poor but Indians are poor. It means that the country has enough money for the development but corrupt politicians and officers make that money as black money and as a result the public has the lack of money and they become poor.

The Indian youth have very much the potential if we look upon the migration ratio of young Indian students and professionals after the engineering and management studies. It is quite surprising that the top students of IITs and IIMs go to foreign countries because they are getting better salary packages there, in turn these bright minded youth help a lot in the development of various fields in those foreign countries. The demand of Indian software engineer is very high in the countries like USA, UK, Canada and Singapore, so you can imagine how much talent and potential these young Indian professionals has? Many young Indian scientists are working in NASA and as we all know that two of NASA based Indian astronauts Kalpana Chawla and Sunita Williams went to space also with the team of NASA astronauts. Thus the matter of fact is Indian young minds have better skills and talent in various fields and if they get better opportunity in their own country the migration of young minds will reduce to much extent. If they get paid according to their skills and contribute towards the organization then they will not leave their motherland whereas they will work for their own country. For any country the youth resource is the best resource and fortunately here in India we don't have lack of this youth resource. The youth have the ability to change the system into best suited for all people. A young leader is the role model of thousands of young people. Currently in India many youth organizations are running and they are doing great job for the welfare of the country. One such organization is Teach for India. This youth driven organization is doing an excellent work by teaching underprivileged children. Many young graduates of India joined this organization under fellowship programme and as a volunteer to in-light the life of thousands of under privileged children in various cities of India.

Now-withstanding, in the present study the constellation of questions have been put to our research participants to ascertain and investigate some of the key reasons and factors behind the challenge to youth in Kashmir. To begin with, we have ascertained certain sociological variables including age, gender, parental education, family income, family pattern etc. of our research participants. It largely held that for an understanding of attitudes, aspirations, social behaviour and overall social makeup of a person, these sociological variables are imperative to be ascertained. Accordingly in the present study certain associations have been made with these background variables to know how the different locations in social structure determines variation in the youth behaviour construction of our respondents and then coupled to the broader issue of youth challenges in the urban and rural settings.

Demographic Sketch

Almost one in five persons in the world is aged between 15 and 24, the majority living in developing countries. India has the largest youth population in the world; around 66 per cent of the total population (more than 808 million) is below the age of 35. Nearly 40 per cent of the Indian population is aged 13 to 35 years (defined as youth in the National Youth Policy). The median age in India in 2010 was just 25.2 years, compared to 34.5 years in China. The Indian labour force is set to grow by over 8 million per annum over the coming decade, most of which will be driven by youth entering the labour market. This is a major challenge for policymakers in terms of creating decent work for the increasingly educated cohorts. Globally youth are three times more likely than adults to be unemployed. Young women typically experience higher rates of unemployment than men. Young people around the world were hit hardest during the global financial crisis due to their precariousness in the labour market. Most young people in developing countries such as India cannot afford to remain unemployed for long but, at the same time, struggle to find decent jobs in the formal economy. Consequently, most youth are underemployed and eking out a living in the informal sector.

Youth structure will define India's future in the socio-economic and political realms, and its experiences will largely determine India's achievement of its goal of population stabilization and the extent to which the nation will be able to harness its demographic dividend. While today's youth are healthier, more urbanized and better educated than earlier generations, social and economic vulnerabilities persist. In the course of the transition to adulthood, moreover, young people face significant risks related to sexual and reproductive health, and many lack the knowledge and power to make informed sexual and reproductive choices. In recognition of the importance of investing in young people, several national policies and programmes formulated since 2000, including the National Population Policy 2000, the National Youth Policy 2003, the Tenth and Eleventh Five-Year Plans, the National Adolescent Reproductive and Sexual Health Strategy and the National Rural Health Mission, have underscored a commitment to addressing the multiple needs of this group in India. Effective implementation of both policies and programmes, however, has been handicapped by the lack of evidence on young people's situation and needs. Currently available evidence is limited, at best, and comes largely from small-scale and unrepresentative studies.

This is the first-ever study conducted to fill these gaps in evidence from Kashmir. Its objectives were to identify key transitions experienced by youth, including those pertaining to education, political participation, economic aspects, work force participation, sexual activity, marriage, health, leisure and entertainment, and civic participation; provide evidence on the magnitude and patterns of young people's political understanding, sexual and reproductive practices in and outside of marriage as well as related knowledge, decision-making and attitudes; and, finally, identify key factors underlying young people's sports and games behaviour, sexual and reproductive health knowledge, attitudes and life choices.

Age and Sex Composition of Population

It is a well-established fact that age plays a dominant role in shaping personality and values of responsibility to work, family, marriage, neighbourhood, community, society etc. and to participate in different walks of life. Surveys published by ILO reveal that the total number of working youth increased dramatically, and working girls outnumbered working boys below fifteen years of age. Between 1971 and 1981 there was an increase in the work participation rate of girls and a decrease in the case of boys (World of Work, 1996). The age distribution of the state of Jammu and Kashmir is typical of a population in which fertility has been declining in the recent past. A little over one-fifth (22%) of the population is aged 0–9 years, and at the other end of the age spectrum, the population aged 60+ years represented 9 per cent. The latest Census report suggest, moreover, that the proportion of the population aged 0–4 years was similar to that observed in the 2001 census in the state (10.0 and 10.7 respectively), and the median age of the population is slightly higher than that reported in the 2001 Census (24 years versus 22.6 years). It was in the above mentioned context that sex and age group of the person was given an important position in the present study. Age and sex composition of the sampled youth are shown in the following Table 5.1.

Table 5.1 gives a panoramic view of the sampled youth population in the valley of Kashmir for the youth study. Utmost care was taken to give equal representation to age as well as sex so that perspectives of different age groups of boys and girls and men and women as shown in the table about youth and youth related issues will come forth. Age groups 19-22 and 23-27 was deliberately given more representation because of being in the fertile period of youth as well as in the peak of their career. With regard to the population of young people, the distribution suggests 11.4 per cent of the population is aged 10–14 years, 9.5 per cent is aged 15–19 years and 8.6 per cent is

Table 5.1: Age and Sex Composition of the Sampled Youth

Age	*Sex (%)*		*Total*
	Boys	*Girls*	
14-18 Years	110 (11.00)	70 (7.00)	180 (18.00)
19-22 Years	160 (16.00)	130 (13.00)	290 (29.00)
23-27 Years	120 (12.00)	160 (16.00)	280 (28.00)
28-31 Years	75 (7.50)	65 (6.50)	140 (14.00)
32-35 Years	70 (7.00)	40 (4.00)	110 (11.00)
Total	535 (53.5)	465 (46.5)	1000 (100)

Source: Field Study.

aged 20–24 years. A total of 18.1 per cent of the population is aged 15–24 years, about the same as that observed in the 2001 Census (18.3%). The sex ratio of the Jammu and Kashmir population is 883 females per 1,000 males, lower than the national average.

Education and Opportunity

Education is of paramount importance for the proper growth and development of the individual. It plays an important role in one's life in the sense that it helps in shaping the right kind of life style in the human beings. It is education which turns children into a social and human being. Education, formal or informal aims at developing the positive quality of the child and helps the individual realize his/her potentialities. While youth in the country were better educated than the general population, schooling was far from universal among them. Research shows, moreover, that young girls in rural areas were particularly disadvantaged; about 5-8 per cent of rural young women and men had never been to school in India.

As mentioned earlier, a total of 1000 youth were interviewed. Age profiles suggest that a somewhat larger proportion of young men and women were concentrated in the 15–25 than in the 26–35 age groups. Caste-wise distributions were generally similar among young men and women. Most of the youth when contacted for the study had both parents surviving. For those with just one parent surviving (very less percentage), this parent was more likely to be the mother (11%) than the father (3–4%). Finally, 1–2% reported that neither parent was alive. The educational profile of the population highlights low levels of educational attainment. Reaffirming the low levels of educational attainment in the population covered by the study, findings also indicate that less than 50 per cent of the total population had received 20 or more years of education, including 35 per cent and 45 per cent of females and males, respectively.

Table 5.2 presents the abridgment of respondents according to their school, college, educational institution, area and by

Table 5.2: Classification of Sampled Youth by School, College, Education, Profession, Occupation and Area

Profession/ Occupation Education	*Place/School/College*										*Total*
	Urban (%)					*Rural (%)*					
	A	*B*	*C*	*D*	*E*	*F*	*G*	*H*	*I*	*J*	
9th -10th	8 (7.27)	12 (9.23)	9 (9.0)	11 (9.56)	7 (6.66)	11 (12.22)	10 (12.5)	10 (11.11)	8 (11.25)	10 (11.11)	96 (9.6)
11th -12th	13 (11.81)	13 (10.0)	14 (14.0)	13 (11.30)	14 (13.33)	10 (11.11)	12 (15.0)	11 (12.22)	12 (15.0)	13 (14.44)	125 (12.5)
1st -2nd Year	17 (17.27)	14 (10.76)	16 (16.0)	15 (13.04)	17 (16.19)	8 (8.88)	9 (11.25)	7 (7.77)	6 (7.5)	9 (10.0)	118 (11.8)
Graduate	22 (20.00)	13 (10.0)	7 (7.0)	16 (13.91)	16 (15.23)	8 (8.88)	10 (12.5)	9 (10.00)	8 (10.0)	10 (11.11)	119 (11.9)
Post Graduate	15 (13.63)	15 (11.53)	22 (22.0)	8 (6.95)	16 (15.23)	9 (10.0)	8 (10.0)	8 (8.88)	8 (10.0)	9 (10.0)	118 (11.8)
Doctorate	3 (2.72)	4 (3.07)	3 (3.0)	4 (3.47)	4 (3.80)	1 (1.11)	0 (0.0)	2 (2.22)	0 (0.0)	0 (0.0)	21 (2.1)
Business	5 (4.54)	11 (8.46)	4 (4.0)	12 (10.43)	4 (3.80)	11 (12.22)	9 (11.25)	10 (11.11)	10 (12.5)	8 (8.88)	84 (8.4)
Govt. Job	6 (5.45)	12 (9.23)	3 (3.0)	8 (6.95)	3 (2.85)	7 (7.77)	4 (5.0)	8 (8.88)	6 (7.5)	9 (10.0)	66 (76.6)
Private Job	6 (5.45)	13 (10.0)	7 (7.0)	12 (10.43)	11 (10.47)	8 (8.88)	6 (7.5)	6 (6.66)	8 (10.0)	10 (1.11)	87 (8.7)
Unemployed	9 (8.18)	14 (10.76)	9 (9.0)	8 (6.95)	6 (5.71)	9 (10.0)	7 (8.75)	11 (12.22)	8 (10.0)	8 (8.88)	89 (8.9)
Self Employed	6 (5.45)	9 (6.92)	6 (6.0)	8 (6.95)	7 (6.66)	8 (8.88)	9 (11.25)	8 (8.88)	6 (7.5)	4 (4.44)	71 (7.1)
Total	110 (11.0)	130 (13.0)	100 (10.0)	115 (11.5)	105 (10.5)	90 (9.0)	80 (8.0)	90 (9.0)	80 (8.0)	90 (9.0)	1000 (100)
	Total Urban = 560					Total Rural= 440					

Source: Field Study.
Note: A,B,C,D,E,F,G,H,I, and J represent sampled areas of the Study.

class of study if a student and also by profession: business, private job, govt. job, self-employed etc. Chemical analysis of data advocates that the representation of youth is almost from every sector of the universe. Comparatively, from all areas of study research participants are approximately in equal proportion. As discussed in methodology section, the rationale for selecting more samples from students of various educational institutions both private and public and graduate and postgraduate is that most of the youth of the valley are studying in these educational institutions. Therefore, it became precondition to have this unbalanced sample in terms of place/ location. Scrutinizing the data on school/college/area-wise basis, we are attuned to a very mixed picture.

Attainment of educational milestones also varied. In total, just two in five young men and two in three young women had completed bachelors' degree. The rates were particularly low among several sub-groups of youth—young women, married youth, downtown youth, those belonging to poor households, and those belonging to lower castes. Among those who had ever enrolled in school/college, substantial declines in school/college completion rates took place earlier among young women than men, the married than the unmarried, and the rural compared to the urban. Moreover, in all groups and all areas, major declines occurred just prior to the bachelor degree completion as well as following the completion of such milestones as a secondary, higher secondary and college education. The leading reason for less attending school among young men and women was economic (for example, the respondent was required for work on the family farm/business or for outside wage earning work, or the family could not afford school-related expenses), reported by about three in five young men and women. More than half of young women, moreover, reported reasons related to housework (the respondent was required for care of siblings or housework). Attitude or perception-related reasons (for example, education was unnecessary or the respondent was not interested in schooling) were other important reasons for rarely going to school, reported by one-third of young men and women. Finally, college/school-related reasons (college/school located too far away, poor school quality and so on) were important, particularly among young women. Among those who had ever been to school, gender differences in reasons for discontinuation became more apparent. Leading reasons for discontinuation among young men, irrespective of the level at which schooling had been discontinued, continued to be economic and attitude and perception-related, and at higher levels, school-related as well. For young women, while percentages differed, leading reasons were economic, attitude- or perception-related, housework responsibilities and college/ school-related. Among young women, moreover, reasons relating to transitions to adult roles, overwhelmingly marriage became increasingly important among those who had discontinued their education at the college level. Of note, particularly, is that one in seven and one in four young women who had discontinued their education in bachelors programme, reported reasons related to transitions to adult roles, notably marriage.

For the most part, youth attended private, co-educational and government schools and colleges. A gender divide was, however, observed in the type of educational facility they attended. While young men, by and large, attended co-educational facilities at all levels of education, percentages of young women attending a co-educational facility declined with level of schooling attained. Moreover, percentages of young men and women attending private educational facilities increased with level of education. As far as availability of such amenities as drinking water, playgrounds, toilets and libraries was concerned, almost all youth had access to drinking water and considerable majorities had no playgrounds. Toilets and library facilities were less likely to be reported by youth, irrespective of their schooling status at the time of the interview. By and large, differences were observed in the availability of amenities at educational institutions attended by youth who were still in school and those who had discontinued their education at various levels. Schooling experiences were relatively similar among young men and women but differed somewhat among those who had discontinued schooling and those who were studying at the time of the interview. While differences in regular attendance and perceptions about academic load were less consistent, youth who were continuing their education were considerably more likely to report private tuition, and to have passed the last examination for which they had appeared. It would appear that academic failure was an important factor precipitating school discontinuation.

Family, Friends and Community Life

Family and community relations were (and remain) the most conservative areas of Kashmiri society. Even in urban settings and cities, amongst the most educated and travelled groups, there was relatively little structural change during the period between 1950s to 2000s; in rural areas, social conventions were even more strongly preserved. Hence, there were perceptible continuities with the pre-conflict period. The extended family networks remained powerful. The actual size of cohabiting units fell sharply, owing to such pressures as the nature and availability of accommodation, changes in employment patterns (including off course, collectivization) and the general regimentation and homogenization of life under religious and cultural domination. Nevertheless, close contact was retained amongst the members of the larger family even they were physically dispersed frequent (in whatever way possible) visits and through other means of communication. In accordance with the Islamic percept, 'Happiness lies at the feet of the mother', sons treated their mothers with huge respect, regarding her every word as a sacrosanct command. This honoured status gave as great a degree of control over their lives, and over the lives of their dependents, as she herself wished to exercise. Within the family unit there is a high degree of order. This expressed itself through a strong, almost ritualized, code of civility which regulated every aspect of behaviour. Children are socialized in the environment to accept their place in the hierarchical structure, with the attendant obligations, responsibilities and privileges. Constructions of masculinity and femininity are internalized at this stage and gender roles assigned. A strong sense of sibling solidarity is fostered, as well as respect and affection for the older members of the family. Habits of obedience, conformity and submission are fostered in girls and boys alike; the later may have had greater freedom of action outside the home, but within the family both genders are equally bound by strict conventions. Though there is still a residential preference for sons, in terms of care, affection and opportunities, daughters no longer appeared to be less privileged than sons.

Employment and Unemployment

Although significant numbers of young people encounter difficulties in making transitions from education to work, relatively few are locked out of the labour market in the long term. Early careers are frequently characterized by regular job changing, sometimes out of necessity as employment is brought to an end by an employer, and at other times out of choice as young workers move jobs to improve pay and conditions, to obtain greater security or career enhancement or simply to take up a job that is more aligned with their interests, skills and qualifications.

The experience of unemployment or being workless is having far-reaching consequences for individuals: it shakes confidence and self-esteem and has been associated with a range of psycho-social disorders. Unemployment also affect relationships with family and friends, lead to isolation and extreme boredom and sometimes lead young to consider alternative, occasionally illegal, ways of making money. Financial hardship shapes the experience, and in families and households where support measures are generous, the consequences of unemployment are less severe. If we have a look on the bad habits spreading among the youth, the data is quite high and it is increasing day by day. The main reasons for indulging in bad habits are bad company of friends and bad environment around the person. Thus the point is that young people have so much of potential that if they use it in constructive work they can lead our society in a path of continuous progress and if they use it in destructive work they may destroy their own and others life too. Therefore the youth of our society have to realize to use their potential in constructive work and in the development of our society. Work profiles suggest that over two-thirds of young men and one-half of young women had at some time engaged in paid or unpaid work. Economic activity was often initiated at an early age: over one in four young men and women reported initiating work in childhood or early adolescence (by age 20). Data on work participation indicate that the majority of young men (61% of unmarried and 97% of married) and a substantial proportion of young women (37% and 43%, respectively) had engaged in paid or unpaid work at some point in last couple of years. The study also reveals substantial levels of unemployment among youth: 44 per cent among young men and 66 per cent among young women. Unemployment was particularly high among the educated—young men and women who had completed Class 12 and BA reported considerably higher rates of unemployment than those who had completed fewer years of schooling. Youth were clearly interested in acquiring skills that would enable employment generation; over half of young men and two-thirds of young women reported interest in vocational skills training. However, far fewer—just 21 per cent of young men and 25 per cent of young women—had attended at least one vocational training programme. Youth in downtown and other sensitive areas were less likely than their other counterparts to have ever attended vocational training programmes. While this locality pattern was not as consistently observed with regard to young people's interest in attending vocational training programmes in general.

Media Exposure

The study reveals that large proportions of youth were exposed to the media, typically television (89% of all young men and 76% of all young women), and, among youth with ten or more years of education, newspapers, magazines or books (93% of young men and 78% of young women). Exposure to the internet, among those with five or more years of education, was reported by considerably fewer youth (15% of young men and 9% of young women). Gender differences were apparent, with young men typically more likely to be exposed to each medium than young women. Region wise differences were narrow with regard to exposure to the print media, but wider in the case of the remaining two media; youth in civil lines and the posh areas, by and large, more likely than their counterparts to report exposure to television and the internet. Findings also suggest that about one in three young men (35%) and hardly any (3%) young women watched pornographic films; 23 per cent of young men and 5 per cent of young women accessed pornographic books and magazines and 37 per cent of young men and 5 per cent of young women who had been exposed to the internet had accessed pornographic materials on the internet. Region-level differences were inconsistent but highlight that young men in civil lines and the posh colonies were more likely than those in the downtown to report exposure to pornographic materials. Finally, between half and three-fifths of young men and women (54–62%) acknowledged the influence that media have on youth behaviours, in terms of influencing the way youth dress or the extent to which they exhibit aggressive behaviours. The Table 5.3 gives a panoramic view of the youth activities in their spare/leisure time.

Analysis of data on the preference of language for communication in inside and outside of the school shows that majority (55%) of elite school children in Kashmir do communicate in Urdu, whether inside or outside of their school and 23 per cent do speak or interact in English in the same contexts. It is just 21 per cent, who prefer and hinge on their mother tongue-Kashmiri while interacting inside or outside of the school context. This analysis of data confirms the frequency of language use and reveals that it is Urdu language dominating the scene both inside and outside of the school, whether it is to interact with class mates or teachers. However, scrutinizing the data further, shows an appreciable percentage

Table 5.3: Classification of Youth according to Activities in Spare Time and Watching Programmes on TV

Activities	*Mostly*	*Sometimes*	*Never*	*No Opinion*
A Playing some game/sport	324	203	255	218
B Watching television	365	214	187	234
C Listening to music	423	403	110	64
D Reading books/Periodicals/ Magazines	298	144	412	146
E Going out with friends	402	210	301	87
Programmes	*Daily*	*More than once a week*	*Rarely*	*Never*
A News/political debates	199	245	376	180
B Religious and spiritual programmes	110	129	546	215
C Songs/films	523	265	186	26
D Reality shows	120	97	180	603

Source: Field Study.

Table 5.4: Preference of Language for Communication in Inside and Outside college/University/Business/School

Language	*With Teachers (%)*		*With Class Mates (%)*		*Total*
	Inside C/U/B	*Outside C/U/B*	*Inside C/U/B*	*Outside C/U/B*	
English	(20)	(23.5)	(24.5)	(25.2)	(23)
Urdu	(71.5)	(57.3)	(66)	(31.8)	(55)
Kashmiri	(7.9)	(19.1)	(9.4)	(42.8)	(21)
Total	(29.3)	(22.6)	(17.6)	(30.3)	(100)

Source: Field Study.

of elite school children in Kashmir do use English both inside and outside of the school while interacting with their friends or teachers. Conversely, mere 7.9 per cent of school children do communicate in Kashmiri with their teachers inside the schools, followed by 9.4 per cent school children, who communicate in Kashmiri with their class mates inside school. Nevertheless, outside the schools a good percentage (42%) of elite school children does interact with their friends in Kashmiri. Such a preference and frequency of using any language is primarily determined by the comfort-ability that one feels while interacting in any language.

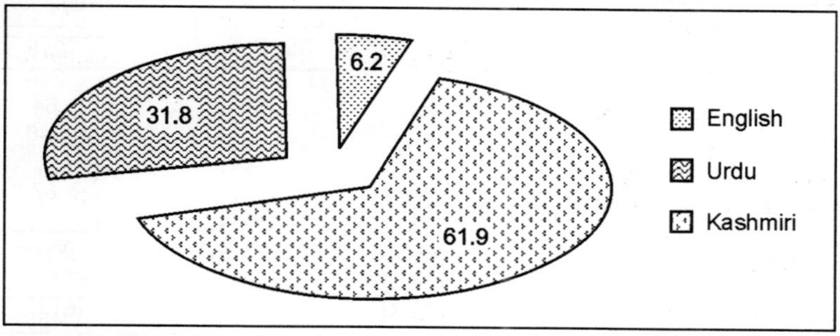

Source: Field Study.

Fig. 5.1: Most Comfortable Language

As many as 61.9 per cent of elite school children in our study viewed Urdu as their most comfortable language for communication (verbal only) whereas just 6.2 per cent of them estimated English as their most comfortable language for interaction. In this connection of level of comfort-ability, albeit next to Urdu, Kashmiri retains some status as 31.8 per cent held it most comfortable language in verbal communication. This pattern of language preference and use in verbal communications is further elaborated by looking at the micro level communications of school children to detect their language use in intimate and formal correspondence out of the school environments.

It is seen from the percentage distribution of data in Table 5.5 that while writing to relatives or friends, 70 per cent youth and children in Kashmir do it through the medium of English, whereas 30 per cent do it in Urdu. Unlike when talking to father and siblings, nearly 51 and 55 per cent respectively do it in Urdu, followed by 37 and 29.3 per cent, who do respectively communicate in Kashmiri with these relatives. In terms of speaking to shopkeeper, 47 per cent school youth and children in Srinagar city do it in Urdu, whereas 49.4 per cent carry in their mother tongue. Together with, it is only in terms of naming days of week, thinking and writing to relatives and friends, wherein English is utilized predominantly. Or else it

Table 5.5: Preference of Using Languages in Intimate and Formal Correspondences

Correspondence	*Languages (%)*		
	English	*Urdu*	*Kashmiri*
Writing to Relatives & Friends	(70)	(30.3)	(3)
Speaking to Father	(11.3)	(51.6)	(37)
Speaking to Siblings	(15.6)	(55)	(29.3)
Speaking to Shopkeeper	(3.6)	(47)	(49.4)
Speaking to Doctor	(4)	(74.3)	(21.6)
Praying to God	(2.3)	(62.6)	(35)
Thinking	(24.3)	(38)	(37.6)
Naming Days of Week	(85.3)	(9.6)	(5)

Source: Field Study.
Note: Percentages for each category of responses are calculated out of total sample

is for the most part Urdu, which is put into practice, followed by Kashmiri. However, the interesting point that needs to be emphasized is that 11.3 per cent elite school children in Kashmir do communicate with their father in English, whilst 15.6 per cent do communicate in English with their siblings. Nonetheless looking at the non-verbal correspondence, as we see above 70 per cent school children in Kashmir do it through the medium of English, is unsurprising given the medium of instruction in elite schools, which is predominantly English. So in terms of written correspondences, one would expect it. However, in terms of other preferences like plays, films, songs, newspapers etc. or what is broadly called mass media, wherein language is the first priority and determinative of the choice i.e. whether to consume English, Kashmiri or Urdu products or content. In this respect the analysis of data in Table 5.6 shows the choices and preference of college/university and school children in Kashmir.

Today it seems natural for us to see the electronic and print media as solidly anchored in the private spheres of our lives. We are all aware that daily newspapers, T.V., radio, internet, computers etc. are most common in our homes and young people are the major consumers and audiences of the mass media. From the above table we could observe that more or

Table 5.6: Preference of Language in Watching TV, Listening Radio and Reading Newspapers and Magazines

Frequency	*Language*	*Watching T.V. (%)*			*Listening Radio (%)*			*Reading (%)*	
		Plays	*News*	*Films*	*Plays*	*News*	*Songs*	*Newspapers*	*Magazines*
Always	Eng.	(4.8)	(6.9)	(2.6)	—	(5.4)	(0.6)	(45)	(38.2)
	Urdu	(64.3)	(68.3)	(90)	(10.3)	(44.5)	(66)	(27.6)	(6.6)
	Kash.	(12.6)	(8)	—	(8.6)	(37.8)	(23.6)	—	—
Sometimes	Eng.	(6.3)	(2.5)	(1.1)	—	(13.4)	(4.6)	(13)	(10.2)
	Urdu	—	(3.3)	—	(81)	—	—	(7)	(25.7)
	Kash	(7)	(4)	—	—	—	(4.3)	—	—
Rarely	Eng.	(1.8)	(6.6)	(6.1)	—	—	(0.6)	—	(5.1)
	Urdu	—	—	—	—	—	—	(7.3)	(13.9)
	Kash	(2.9)	—	—	—	—	—	—	—
	Total	(100)	(100)	(100)	(100)	(100)	(100)	(100)	(100)

Source: Field Study.

Note: Percentages for each category of responses are calculated according to their respective total number.

less every child and young in Kashmir is consuming mass media. Nonetheless, it is the content in Urdu, preferred over and above English and Kashmiri. As regarding watching television, 64.3 per cent said that they always watch Urdu plays, 68.3 per cent always watch Urdu news, whilst 90 per cent always watch Urdu feature films. Just 12.6 youth in urban Srinagar in Kashmir watch Kashmiri plays and 8 per cent watch news in Kashmiri. Likewise, in terms of listening radio, majority go with Urdu as 66 per cent said that they always listen and prefer Urdu songs. In the sphere of reading, however, majority (45%) always read English newspapers, followed by 38.2 per cent, who always read English magazines. Altogether, it is quite apparent from the analysis of data that majority of youth in urban Kashmir prefer to watch and listen Urdu programmes including plays, news, films and songs, which also indicates their penchant for Urdu language. Although, in some spheres like watching/listening plays, songs and news, preference to Kashmiri retains status next to Urdu, but that in no way indicates a healthy trend for Kashmiri language. Unlike in other parts of India first preference is offered to the contents of mass media that are in local indigenous languages.

Youth and Mobile Phones

Human well-being is multidimensional and so requires access to resources to live a good healthy life. Improved human wellbeing is a crucial objective of sustainable development. Sustainable development requires that the needs of the present are met without compromising the ability of future generations to meet their own needs. This type of development takes the impact on the environment into account and tries to minimize environmental damage. Food, income, clean water and energy as well as personal security, good social relations and the opportunity to make a choice are among the lot are factors worth taken into consideration. Thus people are not only physically well but have choices and so live in dignity. The well-being of people affects their ability to effectively and sustainably manage resources. In this respect we cannot ignore the ownership and usage of mobile phones as improvement on communication with others in the society. In 2007 mobile phone technologies were in the hands of almost 3.3 billion people on earth. The widespread diffusion and use of mobile phones is a shift towards a new personal communication society where there are social changes which include new forms of technology and social networking and personalization of public spaces. The widespread diffusion and use of mobile telephony is iconic of a shift toward a new personal communication society evidenced by several key areas of social change including symbolic meaning of the technology, new forms of coordination and social networking, personalization of public spaces, and the mobile youth culture. Like the television in the 1950s and the internet in the 1990s, mobile telephony has emerged as one of the defining communication technologies of our time. Mobile subscriptions are well into the billions worldwide and growing. Not surprisingly, the rapidly increasing adoption and use of mobile communication technology contributes to a host of social consequences, including new representation of the self, new forms of social connection and private use of public space. Some key areas of social change resulting from the widespread adoption and use of mobile telephony and society are considered. It has been argued that the social changes that come out of mobile communication mark a distinctive step in progression from the use of traditional mass media to a new personal communication society.

It was the intention of the study to find out the intrinsic motivation for the adoption of mobile phone technology by youth of Kashmir. This study investigated mobile phone ownership patterns, motivations for mobile phone usage, common usage patterns and the attitudes toward mobile phones among youth of Kashmir. The study was also aimed at assessing the behavioural characteristics in the use of phones by the youth in Kashmiri. The study came out with findings that most respondents used Nokia and Samsung phones because of their quality. The most widely used service providers were BSNL, Airtel, Aircel and Vodafone. Most respondents also bought their phones between Rs. 2000-3000 and most of the phones were bought by youth themselves. A good percentage of youth in Srinagar and other adjoining areas use mobile phones for internet purposes especially to use *Facebook* and some other entertaining and informative websites. The most common billing system used by study participants was the prepaid system with participants recharging weekly and spending less than Rs. 500 per month. The most important reason for purchasing a mobile phone was for the students to remain in easy contact with family and friends. Regarding attitudes most students considered information on their phones to be private. Most of the time the respondents put their phones on silent when they were at lectures (if student) and most could not do without a mobile phone for a day. It is advisable among other things to cut down on the number of times one recharges units to save money and also cut down on the length of time talking on phone in order to have more time for studies as students. Over the years, mobile phones have gone from being expensive equipment used by business elites to a low cost personal item. Most adults and children now own mobile phones. This has made it uncommon to own fixed land lines. With high levels of mobile telephone penetrating, a mobile culture has evolved, where the phone becomes a key social tool and people rely on their mobile phones address book to keep in touch with their friends. Many people keep in touch using SMS and a whole culture of 'texting' has developed from this. The commercial market in SMS is growing. The mobile phone itself has become a totemic and fashion object with users decorating, customizing and accessing their mobile phone to reflect their personality. This has emerged as its own industry.

Youth and Socialization

The present study on youth in Kashmir confirms that puberty occurs in the early teens among both young men and women as in other parts of the world and India. The mean age at menarche is 13.5 years, and young men typically experiencing voice change and the appearance of pubic hair at age 15 according to medical experiments. Findings underscore, in general, the gendered socialization of youth. For example, responses of both young men and women indicate that unequal gender norms regarding freedom of movement prevailed in most study areas, with more than two-thirds of young men acknowledging that they had more freedom to go out than their sisters or female cousins did, and more than eighty per cent of sampled young women agreeing that they had less freedom to go out than their brothers or male cousins. At the same time, more than half of young men and women reported that young men in their family were expected to do less housework than were young women. Findings also suggest that parents controlled both young men's and women's social interactions, particularly those involving members of the opposite-sex: for example, 69 per cent of young men and 82–84 per cent of young women expected parental disapproval if they brought an opposite-sex friend home. Findings regarding communication with parents on issues relevant to youth—such as school performance, romantic relationships, growing up matters and reproductive processes—reiterate those from other studies, showing that such communication is far from universal. Indeed, sensitive topics—such as romantic relationships and reproductive processes—were rarely discussed with either parent, and growing up matters were discussed only by young women with their mother. The Table 5.7 gives a description of the youth believing in the role of elders in different walks of life in the affairs of the youth.

Table 5.7: Description of Youth who Believe in the Role of Elders in the Affairs of the Youth

	Role of Elders	*Great extent*	*Somewhat*	*Not at all*	*No opinion*
A	Moral Guidance	285	332	203	180
B	Religious Guidance	431	208	113	248
C	Cultural role	217	187	202	394
D	Role in Unity and brotherhood	192	190	310	308
E	Role as Models of Tradition	129	336	223	312
F	Linguistic Role	171	398	186	295

Source: Field Study.

The parent-child communication was restricted was also evident from responses to questions probing the most likely confidante on a range of topics from taking a job to boy-girl relationships. While a parent was mentioned as the leading confidante on the subject of taking a job, a parent was rarely cited as a leading confidante on the more sensitive matter of boy-girl relationships. Moreover, while young women identified their mother as the most likely confidante on menstrual problems, young men rarely identified a parent as a leading confidante on matters relating to nocturnal emission. Young people's family lives were marked by violence, both witnessed and experienced. As many as one-quarter of young men and women had observed their father beating their mother. Many respondents reported experiencing a beating by a parent during adolescence; gender differences were marked, with almost half of young men and one-fifth of young women reporting such experiences. The findings of the present study also suggest the familiar rural-urban divide with regard to the growing up experiences of young men and women, although these differences were not consistently observed. Of note were findings that some young men from civil lines and the posh colonies than from the downtown and other sensitive areas perceived approval from their parents if they brought opposite-sex friends home.

Table 5.8: Classification of Youth who Indicate Separate Image of Theirselves than Adult Society

	Adopted image of self	*Great extent*	*Somewhat*	*Not at all*	*No opinion*
A	Idealistic	311	196	137	356
B	Materialistic	559	252	93	96
C	Educationist	233	302	109	356
D	Lazy and Selfishness	187	207	343	263
E	Romantic	275	197	210	218
F	Religious	297	238	210	255

Source: Field Study.

Peer Group Networks and Interaction

Growing-up is associated with close peer group networks. Almost 55 per cent of the sampled youth reported having some same-sex friends. Young men typically reported a somewhat larger network of friends than did young women. Opposite-sex peer networks were less common but nonetheless reported by 27 per cent of young men and 16 per cent of young women. Indeed, findings suggest that youth derived an important measure of support from their peer group networks on personal matters: friends were by far the leading confidante on boy-girl relationships for both young men and women, and on nocturnal emission for young men.

Family, Parental Education and Occupation

Family is the core building block of society. Children's experience of family affects many aspects of their everyday lives, shaping their expectations and future plans. Especially in the countries where, for example, filial piety and joint family are the guiding principles of family and kinship organizations, the socialization of the young is of a different order compared to societies where the nuclear family is the norm. In the latter societies, the young leave their families of orientation to live separately and, thus, attain relative freedom from parental care and control. But in the South Asian countries where the joint family norm still prevails to a large extent, the family of orientation meets the obligation of providing the young with at least every kind of support be it education, employment or any other sphere. In such societies, the functional joint-ness, even where there is physical separation, offers a kind of social security net and there is maximum tendency for individuals to remain close to their culture, traditions and heritage, which includes language as well. Parental education and occupation acts as an influencing factor in the personality development and has also a profound impact on an individual's attitudes and aspirations, because personality variables such as valuation and motivation for any new cultural formation are not independent. Similarly practicing or willing to practice any language other than mother tongue is not independent of cultural context to which the aspirant belongs.

Table 5.9: Family Type and Proficiency in English, Urdu and Kashmiri

Family Type	*Proficiency in English*	*Proficiency in Urdu*	*Proficiency in Kashmiri*	*Total*
Nuclear	(67.4)	(50.9)	(28.8)	(51.3)
Joint	(25.5)	(41.9)	(59.3)	(40.6)
Extended	(6.9)	(7.0)	(11.8)	(8)
Total	(28.6)	(51.6)	(19.6)	(100)

Source: Field Study.

However, contemporarily the family structure in our sub-continent has changed at least at an average level. Indeed there have been fierce debates on the significance of changes in family structures in the Indian context over the last few decades, focussed on the shift from extended to joint to nuclear family, statistical decline in rates of marriage and rise in rates of divorce, cohabitation, and of 'reconstituted' families etc. Many writers, including Bauman (2003), argue that these patterns reflect a decline in commitment to family. Yet, the overall repercussions for socialization and transmission of culture in this process of familial changes remain unnoticed and this is more so in case of Kashmir, where due to the impact of modern social transformations on cultural norms, socialization processes and values are affected. For instance at times the traditional pattern of subordinating when greeting an elder has changed to "hi."

Which familial structures or home environment is more conducive to the socializing of children in a language other than their local? In an answer to this, the analysis of data in Table 5.9 reveals that at surface level, it is nuclear family, where children have been found to have more proficiency in English (67.4%) and Urdu (50.9%) — the languages relatively alien to our traditional day to day living (table). Though to some extent

Urdu was used there as a channel of communication, particularly in the basic language skills of writing and reading, however, it was still the local mother tongue Kashmiri used widely and across populations.

Nevertheless, we could observe from the table that comparatively a small percentage of school children from joint (25.5%) and extended (6.9%) were having proficiency in English language. Rather there was an appreciable percentage (71.1%) of school children collectively from joint and extended families, as per their own estimation were proficient in local Kashmiri language. This gives an amount of evidence to suggest that joint families and extended families are still quite successful in the transmission of traditions and culture to new generation. Arguably, it is the apparent hierarchy of structure, comprising of grandparents, their sons and daughters and then their children etc. that makes this transmission possible in these families, because in a sense, the presence of grandparents means the presence of traditional culture, which for the most part constitutes language.

Thus the absence of such a family structure added by new modern aspirations, which are archetypal to nuclear families may be the reasons of why more and more school children from nuclear families have shown an inclination towards English and Urdu language. As Talcott Parsons (1971) argues that nuclear family is structurally isolated or in other words more specialized to meet the needs of both industry and market. Language in this process is being specifically played. English is the language of globalization and as we are witness to the global economy and culture in Kashmir as well, nuclear families in particular feel forced to prepare their wards in English language so to make crucial alliances with modern industry and technology. In this respect Young and Willmott have long ago argued that the family, industry and technology have achieved mutual adaption. Same has been the case in Kashmir, which like many beautiful, self-sufficient regions in the world, has been impacted by external forces and caused massive and rapid transformations and youth of the valley especially urbanites are dominantly engulfed in it. At the core of this phenomenon are the ongoing process of modernization and the linkage of a traditional subsistence economy to regional and national markets.

Sex, Gender and Youth

The present study clearly highlight young women's limited agency. For example, just one in four young women (27%) reported independent decision-making on all three issues explored in the study, namely, decisions on choice of friends, spending money and purchase of clothes for oneself. Likewise, freedom of movement even within the locality or neighbourhood was not universal among young women; only three-quarters of young women (73%) had the freedom to visit locations within their own locality or neighbourhood unescorted. Moreover, just one-quarter of young women reported freedom to visit at least one place outside the village or neighbourhood unescorted, and 15 per cent could visit a health facility unescorted. Access to and control over financial resources tended to be limited among young women; fewer than two in five reported some savings and 4 in 10 owned a bank savings account. Over 60 per cent young men had opened an account in bank and were having some saving in comparison to the girls. Of those young women who owned an account, just 54 per cent operated it themselves. While in each area, women's agency was limited, a clear area-wise pattern was not discernible. For example, young women from civil lines displayed considerably higher levels of decision-making than did those from the other areas. Also notable from the findings is the striking gender divide in all the dimensions of young people's agency explored in the study. Young women were far more disadvantaged than young men, and this was apparent everywhere. For example, even the least educated young men belonging to the poorest (first) wealth quintile were more likely than the most educated women and those in the wealthiest (fifth) quintile to report independent decision-making on all the three issues explored in the study. Although young women were more likely than young men to have money saved (36% and 23%, respectively), they were slightly less likely than young men to own a bank savings account (11% and 15%, respectively). Moreover, young women were much less likely than their male counterparts to operate these accounts themselves (54% versus 90% of those who had an account).

Knowledge of Sexual and Reproductive Health Matters

The present study underscores young people's limited awareness of most sexual and reproductive matters, ranging from how pregnancy occurs to contraception, HIV and safe sex practices. Although knowledge of the legal minimum age at marriage was reported by large proportions of youth, there is actually a section which either lack information about legal age of marriage or simply doesn't care about it since economic and other social conditions weigh heavily for their survival. Youth had few sources of information on sex and reproduction. Indeed, almost half of young women and one-sixth of young men reported that they had never received any formal information on sexual matters (prior to marriage among the married). Leading sources of information on sexual matters were friends and the media for both young men and women. In contrast, just 10 per cent of young men and women cited teachers and 3–7 per cent cited health care providers as a source of information; just 2 per cent and 9 per cent of young men and women, respectively, cited a family member. Youth were overwhelmingly in favour of the provision of family life or sex education to young people (83% of young men and 78% of young women); typically, young men preferred to receive this education from a teacher, while young women preferred to obtain it from either a family member or a teacher. Research suggest, moreover, that youth who had undergone family life or sex education were indeed more knowledgeable about sexual and reproductive matters than those not exposed to it. Locality pattern was to some extent apparent with respect to young people's levels of awareness about such matters as correct specific knowledge of modern contraceptive methods, the legal minimum age at marriage, and perceptions about the condom.

Youth, Love Affairs and Romantic Relations

The investigation confirms that despite strict norms prohibiting pre-marital opposite-sex mixing, opportunities do exist for the formation of pre-marital romantic relationships. Indeed, significant proportion of young men and women in the urban setting of Kashmir had made or received a "proposal" for a romantic relationship (45–55%), and noteworthy, if smaller, percentages reported that they had been involved in a romantic partnership (35% and 9% of young men and women, respectively). Patterns of pre-marital romantic partnerships suggest that where partnerships occurred, they were initiated at an early age and were usually hidden from parents but not from peers. The majority of youth who engaged in a pre-marital romantic partnership had expectations of a longer-term commitment; young women were considerably more likely than young men to have expected a romantic relationship to lead to marriage (87% and 57%, respectively). The experiences of the married suggest, moreover, a disconnect between intentions and reality: while 64 per cent and 92 per cent of married young men and women who reported a pre-marital romantic partner, respectively, had intended to marry their pre-marital partner, far fewer (23% and 64%, respectively) had done so. There was a clear progression in reported physical intimacy and sexual experience with romantic partners: while 88 per cent of young men had held hands with a romantic partner, no one reported to had sex with their partner; among young women, while three-quarters had held hands with a romantic partner.

Sexual Exploitation and Youth

Every young is likely to experience some difficulties in his/her job/education and most importantly when the candidate is a young fertile female. Some of these difficulties may be of a permanent nature or of casual, temporary and/or occasional types. But the question of fertile young female being sexually exploited remains there always especially in a violent hit and conflict ridden society like Kashmir. Presence of military, army, police and militants have created a big sense of insecurity among youth of the valley and young girls have been raped, molested, sexually assaulted by men in uniform. Parents and close relatives always prefer to keep away their young girls from these people even if it collides with the education of the girl because honour, respect and dignity is first important priority to them. Sexual exploitation may take many forms and is usually under reported and not talked about openly. The overwhelming response of eighty per cent of young girls said yes, that they are very prone to be sexually exploited. Entry of girls especially into market work was not a matter of choice but a matter of economic compulsion, largely to supplement the family's income and to meet ever increasing individual expenses. Majority of the young girls responded that it is mostly the employer and the people they know and people of his relation who are always in search of opportunity for sexual harassment/exploitation.

Marriage and Youth

The field study for the this project gives a detailed picture of the Kashmiri marriage. The research found that men and women married in and around 30's and 35's, following a long engagement. The study found that in the olden days people wed when they even were younger. In 1980's families selected spouses for their children, although sons and daughters were consulted on their preferences at times. Extremely few people never married, as marriage offered social status, companionship, economic cooperation and, for men, legal paternity of their children. Cultural convention strongly discouraged sexual relations before becoming formerly engaged and wedded. By the 2000's marriage pattern had altered dramatically, due primarily to the impact of heavy urbanization, globalization and modernization and emerging levels of outmigration.

Marriage is now delayed until a later age while migrant students and workers might come home between jobs or on vacation, they generally do not settle down until they reach their late twenties and early thirties. Until then, they prefer to continue working as migrants while they gather the financial resources to set up their own household. Today, men marry when they are near thirties, some ten years later than fifty years ago. Even though marriage may be delayed, courting relations and love affairs between men and women flourish. Before the final step of marriage takes place and, frequently, even before an engagement has been formalized, good number of women and men made romance and entertainment themselves with the relationship.

Not only did marriage occur at young ages but it was also often arranged without the participation of young people themselves, particularly young women. Almost all youth reported arranged marriages. As many as one in ten young men and one in four young women reported that their parents did not seek their approval while determining their marriage partner. Hence, not surprisingly, reported pre-marital acquaintance was limited. Just one in five young men and one in seven young women reported that they had ever had a chance to meet and interact with their spouse-to-be alone prior to marriage. But the options of meeting and interacting with the partner before marriage has increased to a considerable extent and majority of the youth engaged for marriage go on date and premarital romance. The study found that urban youth have higher frequency of meeting and interacting with their life partners before marriage. About one in three married youth reported that they had met their spouse for the first time on the wedding day. Compounding the lack of pre-marital acquaintance was the lack of awareness of what to expect of married life, reported by 70 per cent of young men and 78 per cent of young women. Initiation of pre-marital sexual activity increased as young people transitioned from early into late adolescence, and further into young adulthood. We acknowledge that youth, especially young women, may not report their sexual experiences in a study situation. Hence, the

Youth Study supplemented a series of direct questions with an opportunity to report sexual experiences in an anonymous format. Overall; it would appear that the technique did not indeed offer a considerable number of sexually active young men and women who opted not to disclose their sexual experiences in face-to-face questioning the opportunity to do so.

Despite the existence of laws against the payment of dowry, this practice characterized the marriages of about three-quarters of young men (72%) and women (78%). Findings also show that families of urban youth were as likely as their rural counterparts to conform to traditional practices, such as the payment of dowry. Reports of marital life suggest that spousal communication was far from universal and that marital life was marked by considerable violence. While the Youth Study did not explore extra-marital sexual experiences in detail, the available data indicate that 4 per cent of young men reported an extra-marital sexual encounter. In contrast, hardly any young women reported so.

Health, Substance/Drug Use and Well Being

Although youth is a generally healthy period of life, significant respondents reported experiencing general, mental, and sexual and reproductive health problems. For example, responses indicative of mental health disorders were reported by seven in twelve young men and women. With regard to care seeking for general and sexual and reproductive health problems, patterns varied by type of problem. Of those who had sought treatment, large proportions of young men and women had sought advice or treatment in a very informal way and private facility or provider, irrespective of the type of problem. Findings suggest that youth were shy about seeking sexual and reproductive health services. For example, many youth, including the married, reported that they would indeed hesitate to approach a health care provider or a pharmacy/medical shop for contraceptive supplies.

Findings show that substantial proportions of young men reported the consumption of drugs, tobacco and alcohol; almost one-third of young men reported tobacco consumption and one-sixth reported alcohol consumption. As expected, few young women reported that they had consumed any of these substances. In contrast, hardly any young men and not a single young woman reported drug use.

6

Conflict, Youth and Governance

Societies are affected significantly and crucially due to conflicts. Be it ethnic conflict, religious conflict, historical conflict, regional conflict or political conflict, has affected millions of people and resulted in loss of human lives, destruction of public or Government property, loss of livelihood, loss of opportunity in terms of economic growth and human development, thus involving significant private and social cost. Research in this direction have helped to identify problems which are directly or indirectly affecting the societies facing conflict situation. The massive destruction and change of social fabric due to conflict affects young people to even higher degree than other sectors of society. Youth are uniquely affected by conflict and threats to their security. They are vulnerable as both victims and perpetrators of violence. Conflict impacts negatively on all dimensions of their lives. Conflict remains one of the leading causes of death for youth and young adults. In many parts of the world, the loss of life in countries affected by armed conflict is high, particularly for the youth. Adolescence and youth are a critical stage in a person's development. It is a time of rapid transformation which can see young people taking risks as they try on their new roles and responsibilities. This period is intensified during times of conflict when the social norms and means of support are removed, stopping young people from making a normal evolution to becoming an adult.

The armed conflict in Kashmir which started in 1989, have a devastating impact upon the well-being of the civilian population, particularly women, children and youth. There is

Table 6.1: Classification of Youth who have Participated in any Protest, Demonstration or Movement and Interest in Politics

Reason	*Frequently*	*Sometimes*	*Never*	*No opinion*
a) Your Religion	344	234	287	135
b) Your State of Origin/ Region	509	229	194	66
c) Your Gender	231	324	321	124
d) Economic Status	163	243	398	196
		Interest in Politics		
Very interested	*Somewhat interested*	*Not very interested*	*Not at all interested*	*No opinion*
230	237	243	138	142

Source: Field Study.

hardly any sphere of life which remained unaffected due to this armed conflict. The economy of the state, tourism, agriculture, trade, industry, education, social welfare and health sector all suffered a setback. It has been estimated that around one lakh people mostly youth have lost their lives in this conflict and more than 10 lakhs have been injured. It has also been estimated that about 80,000 children have been orphaned as a result of conflict. The number of persons disappeared is more than 10,000. The ongoing conflict situation has disturbed all aspects of common Kashmiri's life. The conflict (since 1989) has affected the youth in Kashmir, and draw some logical conclusion in relation to the major themes like, perception of youth about conflict, education, social life, physical health, psychosocial well- being and mental health of youth and how they are coping in conflict situation.

The present study divulges that all the respondents believe that Kashmir is a conflict ridden and violence hit society. Majority of the respondents' shared similar responses that conflict has its history in India's Independence and aftermath. They believe Kashmir conflict as one of the longest running conflicts today. Everyone in Kashmir has been touched by the conflict in some way. The study reveals that majority of the respondents i.e. 89.1 per cent felt that the impact of conflict situation proved pervasive and mostly negative on Kashmiri society. It has created enormous upheaval at the personal, family and societal level. The prolonged period of time the Kashmir has been in conflict, combined with the more recent years of consecutive mass uprisings from 2008 to 2010 provides grim reminder of the reality that human life in Kashmir continues to be deplorable. While the negative repercussions of conflict are rampant, the small percentage of respondents' i.e. (4.5%) was of the opinion that conflict also brought certain significant positive changes. The positive impact of the armed conflict found among young people is increasing awareness on different social, religious, political, economic, and cultural, issues etc. Youths have realized the need to understand and be aware of the politics.

An overwhelming majority of respondents' i.e. (91.8%) don't find Kashmir a safe place to live in. The reasons mentioned by the respondents were: sense of insecurity, uncertainty of life and harassment. Nearly all respondents reported that they are exposed to violence, majority of the respondents (89.3%) faced violence through crackdowns, (after an announcement from mosque loudspeakers all men have to assemble at an open place and then the houses are searched) 93.1 per cent respondents said they are unnecessarily frisked by security forces every now and then. Many times they are forced to get down from buses and private vehicles. 69.3 per cent respondents have faced violence through round up raids (when few houses are surrounded and all family members are asked to stay in one room while the houses are searched.) 61.8 per cent respondents have witnessed the incidents of cross firing and (46.6%) explosion of mines/grenades.

The respondents have experienced many forms of sufferings. A widespread experience of majority of the respondents' i.e. (65.8%) has faced harassment by security forces. The respondents upheld the opinion that daily harassment has become indispensable part of Kashmiri life. From people being frisked, identification parades, untimely cordons and arrests, people in general and youth in particular are made to suffer nuisance. The study further reveals that repercussion of the on-going conflict situation is displacement of youth. 39.7 per cent respondents had to leave their homes

It can be inferred that recent generation of youth have suffered enormously (and continued to do so) in the two-decade long conflict. Among the respondents, male youth tend to have more personal experience of conflict than females, in particular when it comes to being physically tortured and harassed and being injured, arrested and repeated displacement.

Fig. 6.1

subsequently during the outbreaks of violence. The causes of displacement are many, like harassment on part of security agencies; they have been forced involuntarily to relocate due to security measures and other threats imposed by conflict. The respondents at greater percentage have also witnessed the incidents like killings in their family, self-detention, mistreatment and injuries during the on-going conflict. Many youth have become orphaned and have taken on the responsibility to care for younger siblings. This experience was shared by both male and female respondents.

Youth, Civil Society and Political Engagement

Active citizenship involves an awareness of rights and responsibilities and engagement in the life of the community which is in vogue in the urban city. Findings highlight the limited participation of youth in civil society. Although a number of programmes are organized by the government or NGOs at the community level in which youth can participate, few youth (22% of young men and 17% of young women) reported familiarity with these programmes. Even fewer youth—7 per cent of young men and 5 per cent of young women—reported participating in such programmes. Relatively larger proportions of young men (45%) and young women (15%) reported that they had participated in community-led activities such as the celebration of festivals and national days. Finally, just 10–11 per cent of young men and women reported membership in organized groups. They were also more likely to report participation in community-led programmes and membership in organized groups. A similar pattern was observed with regard to the expression of secular attitudes: Youth in civil lines and posh colonies were consistently more likely to express secular attitudes than their downtown counterparts.

Table 6.2: Classification of Youth on the Basis of Trust on the Institutions of the State/Government

	Institutions	*Great deal*	*Somewhat*	*Not at all*	*No opinion*
A	Central Govt.	67	76	615	242
B	State Govt.	295	210	375	120
C	Civil service	269	233	348	150
D	Police	73	127	644	156
E	Army	11	33	832	124
F	Courts	175	257	268	300
G	Political parties	57	168	635	140
H	Election commission	23	59	725	193
I	Panchayats	89	123	52	236

Source: Field Study.

Furthermore the respondents responded to the queries that everyone should be allowed to express his/her opinion, even if majority is of different opinion. Another group of youth believes that the best way to resolve conflict is to opt for violence since they have a faith that revolution is always violent. But at the same time nobody should be allowed to protest if they endanger public property responded another group of youth including both boys and girls especially girls from the city of Srinagar.

Research suggest that large proportions of youth did not indeed vote, and however voting behaviour was far from universal about who voted. Large majorities of youth (83–86%) perceived that one could not vote freely and without fear and pressure. At the same time, however, considerable proportions reported dissatisfaction with the political process: 68 per cent of young men and 57 per cent of young women reported disillusionment with the commitment of political parties to work for change at the community level.

Table 6.3: Classification of Youth who have Casted Votes and their Belief that Votes have effect on the Governance and Administration

Casting a vote	*Frequency*	*Votes make a difference*	*Frequency*
A Voted in every election	38	Has effect	75
B Voted in most of the elections	55	Makes no difference	436
C Hardly ever voted	583	No opinion	489
D No opinion	233		
E Eligible only once	91		

Source: Field Study.

Regional patterns were heavily evident with regard to political participation. However, majority of youth from the valley perceive that one could not vote freely and without fear or pressure. Considerable proportions of youth from all the regions reported disillusionment with the political process. About three-fifths (63%) of young men and half (51%) of young women reported that they would mix freely with individuals of different religions and castes, would eat together with a person of a different caste or religion, and would talk to a person who has had an inter-caste marriage. Findings suggest a consistent positive association between age, education and wealth status, and expression of secular attitudes. Considerable proportions of young men and women acknowledged that physical fights among young men and also among young women did occur in their neighbourhood; however, just 11 per cent of young men and 3 per cent of young women reported that they had been involved in a physical fight.

Table 6.4: Classification of Youth on the Basis of Agreement and Disagreement over the following Statements

Statements	*Agree*		*Disagree*		*No opinion*
	Strongly	*Some-what*	*Strongly*	*Some-what*	
A Politicians don't care about people like me	322	255	122	47	144
B Political parties are necessary in democracy	123	156	95	133	493
C It is citizens duty to vote during elections	118	252	197	119	314
D In J&K power rests with people	55	39	531	211	142
E I find politics too complicated	213	197	312	223	57

Source: Field Study.

The six leading problems facing youth expressed by both young men and women were unemployment, violence and security, political disturbance, poverty, lack of amenities and lack of educational opportunities. However, young people's perceptions of these problems varied enormously by sex. Among young men, the majority reported difficulty in finding employment as the leading problem, followed by sense of insecurity and threat to life and survival, concerns about poverty more generally, lack of amenities or infrastructure and lack of educational opportunities. In contrast, the leading problem expressed by young women was lack of amenities and infrastructure, cultural and religious restrictions on movement and mobility as well curb on their movement due to military presence and to a lesser extent, difficulty in finding employment, poverty more generally, and lack of opportunities for education.

There is a need of change in the political culture of the State; for people to think of themselves as active citizens, willing, able and equipped to have an influence in public life and with the critical capacities to weigh evidence before speaking and acting; to build on and radically extend to young people the best in existing traditions of volunteering and public

Table 6.5: Classification of Sampled Youth by Priority to Different Aspects

	Statements	*Very important*	*Somewhat important*	*Not important at all*	*No opinion*
A	Dressing in Latest Style/ trends	485	230	78	110
B	Being Interested in Politics	180	205	395	220
C	Taking on Responsibility	380	290	85	255
D	Getting Higher Education	473	126	201	199

Source: Field Study.

service, and to make them individually confident in finding new forms among themselves.

Socio-Psychological Impact of Conflict on Youth

There is a substantial overlap in the populations having serious psychological distress and who experienced a major depressive episode, but meeting criteria for psychological distress indicates that the respondent exhibited a high level of distress due to any type of mental problem including general symptoms related to phobia, anxiety and depression. The depression corollared out of the impact of conflict on one member of the family for whatever reasons has left a deep imprint on the minds and hearts of already homesick women and children in particular on those born after 1989. In such conditions the psychological disturbance will not only put a ceiling on the innovative and out of box ideas and solutions for the better management of the domestic business but will also lead to a devastating effect on the upbringing of the children and their schooling. This in turn produced children of depression and disturbance which continuously affect their psyche unless something different and unique is not put into practice.

The findings also revealed that respondents have many fears resulting from the traumatic events around them. The major fear mentioned by majority of the respondents (81%) was to live with uncertainty. The respondents stated that they were susceptible to wide range of immediate and long term threats to personal safety. In the absence of peace the

Table 6.6: Description of Insecurity and Anxiety Among Youth

Insecurities/anxiety		Great extent	Somewhat	Not at all	No opinion
A	Riots and mob violence in the State	422	232	123	223
B	employment/career	633	180	73	114
C	Prospects of marriage	170	217	242	271
D	Issues within family	195	201	324	280
E	Militancy and terrorism in the state	189	236	210	365
F	Personal health problems	96	198	418	188

Source: Field Study.

respondents continued to live with fears of outbreak of violence and insecurity. They are being constantly worried and uncertain over their future. Near about 73 per cent respondents particularly fear losing a loved one. Along these immediate practical issues, there are also emotional factors, being humiliated is something that respondents fear in significant numbers (54%) respectively. Other common fears include economic hardships (33%) sexual violence (26%), imprisonment (19%) and being separated from loved ones (12%). Male and female respondents shared very similar fears; with only slight differences of emphasis (e.g. males have more fear of imprisonment, females of losing a loved one. Fear of sexual violence is higher among females than males, but certainly not confined to females alone. This level of fear is also found among male respondents. This indicates that these tendencies (high degree of fear and hostility which is prevalent among the most vulnerable section of the society) are very unhealthy for any society.

The statistical figures while assessing the psychosocial problems faced by respondents, displayed a clear and tremendous effect. The respondents have faced multiple psychosocial problems in which majority i.e. 72 per cent respondents expressed serious psychological and social difficulties such as hopelessness and helplessness and profound social alienation as a result of the on-going violence and deprivation they had experienced during the last few years. It was found that fear of life being ended anywhere created a sense of helplessness among respondents. 62 per cent respondents are easily frightened. Nearly half of the respondents, 48 per cent didn't enjoy their daily activities. We also find other problems like loss of interest in life, sleeping disturbance, lack of concentration in studies, aggressive behaviour, thought of ending life etc. at greater percentage. The results of the study have indicated that exposure to physical traumatic component (experience/witnessed physical violence and torture, experienced a life threatening event) to be the strong indicator for damaging psychosocial well-being. While assessing about the impact of their psychosocial problems on the respondents' general health, the respondents were found to have multiple physical health problems Where body pains rated highest (37%) followed by chest pain (23%) and the underlying cause is emotional trauma. Besides other physical health problems like abdominal complaints, heart pain and headache were also found in the present study.

The coping mechanism repeatedly mentioned by the majority of the respondents was faith in Islam and God, and the support of peer groups. Religion was said to be the most important coping mechanism for majority (38%) of the respondents, their faith in God and Prayer helped them get over their fears. 23 per cent respondents sought help and support from their friends and family, when they feel disturbed or upset. Other coping mechanisms mentioned by the respondents were, visit to faith healers, isolate and keep themselves busy, taking antidepressants etc. in times of stress. Further the respondents who have become victims during conflict showed grievances towards Govt. as they had not received any help and support from Govt. or any NGOs.

Socio-Economic Impact of Conflict on Youth

While assessing the impact on education of youth, it has come to fore that this aspect has been tremendously affected due to conflict. The study reveals high percentage of respondents (83%) have missed out classes in their colleges due to frequent strikes and curfews and 68 per cent respondents conveyed that quality and effectiveness of education also deteriorated severely over the last years. The respondents reported that most of their peers left education in a midway because of the interrupted education or lack of income, while many others migrated to other parts of India and abroad. Further the activities like student union and discussion forums were found non available in colleges, the respondents also conveyed that their educational institutions don't promote any student participation and decision making at any level. The greater percentage of respondents (76.8%) did not have any regular interactions and exchanges with students from other local and non-local colleges. The respondents further complained about the non-availability of facilities of internet services in their respective educational institutions. Some of the respondents have missed out their school or college education for one or more years. The reasons of disruption in their studies mentioned by the respondents were detention and lack of economic resources.

Table 6.7: Classification of Youth Experiencing Discrimination on Various Accounts in Day-to-Day Life Within and Outside the State

Reason	*Frequently*	*Sometimes*	*Never*	*No opinion*
A Your Religion	430	210	90	260
B Your Caste	180	210	230	370
C Your State of Origin/Region	530	265	47	138
D Your Gender	335	223	210	105
E Economic Status	405	209	110	276

Source: Field Study.

While probing into the educational and employment opportunities, the study reveals that only 3 per cent respondents avail scholarships for their studies while a huge 97 per cent have to wholly finance their own education. The same table reveals that, a huge 82 per cent claimed that they didn't enjoy their studies and about a mere 18 per cent said they did. The reasons for not enjoying the studies mentioned by the respondents were: (a) lack of exposure, (b) lot of new courses outside are not available here, (c) communication gap between teachers and students, (d) no guest lectures in their respective educational institutions. Further it was found that due to the atmosphere of uncertainty and fear and interrupted college, the students did not enjoy their studies and it was evident from the level of involvement among students on campuses. Also, the visible trauma due to violence is a factor which somewhat supports the above claim. The statistics in the study further revealed that, among the students, a huge 82 per cent fear that their education is not going to help them find a job in future. Most of the respondents were interesting in going outside valley. They felt anxious about their future given the absence of prospective jobs in the Valley. Given the circumstances, the respondents were skeptical about future. It was observed that in the present context, even the smallest positive elements have been reduced to pessimism and this includes education which does not seem to provide any hope to young people in Kashmir.

On assessing the impact of conflict on social life of youth, it was perceived that conflict has influenced their social life to great extent. The presence of a large number of security forces has created serious obstacles in their social life. Their families also hardly allow them to visit their friends or participate in extracurricular activities due to the persistent security threat. There are always restrictions and impositions on their life conveyed the respondents. The female respondents explicitly were more of concern than boys regarding the frequent college closures due to curfews and strikes as they consider college a place for socialization. It was also found that due to strikes and curfews for months the students have been deprived of the simple yet joyful experiences of college life and this loss has had its impact on their lives.

Leisure, Conflict and Youth

The study reveals that conflict has hindered the ability of the young to enjoy and play activities in the company of peers. The respondents reported that there are no recreation centers or community halls in their respective colleges, while these privileges are available to most institutions in other parts of

India. Young people feel caged at their homes and feel that over the years they have become habituated to remain at home. Majority of the respondents (71%) spent their free time in watching T.V., 68 per cent respondents surf internet in their leisure time. It was observed that the internet has become a window to the world for Kashmiri youth, whose lives are already over-ridden by restrictions on movement and social interaction. It brought in a range of opportunities and helped to explore alternative lives. The youth spent their most of the leisure time on social networking sites like Facebook, Orkut, YouTube and many such web platforms to interact with their friends and relatives. 51 per cent respondents preferred reading books, another 21 per cent respondents said they spent their free time in searching employment.

Majority of the 67.5 per cent respondents revealed their opinion that conflict situation in Kashmir has certainly contributed to the emergence of late marriage. (32.3%) respondents gave reason that conflict created a situation of general unemployment and poverty which has resulted in late marriage. Youth have difficulty in getting married in Kashmir, unless they are in some form of government employment or the other. Financial security is the single most important concern of Kashmiri's and government. Employment is viewed as the lone option of providing that. Kashmiri society does not appreciate anything other than government jobs and only people in those jobs are given respect. This is a major deterrent. Majority of the respondents i.e. 93.1 per cent in the study claimed that they regularly listened to or watched news programmes. The high viewership explains that the present situation is of serious concern to the students. The study further revealed that 51.4 per cent respondents have participated in street protests, the reasons mentioned by respondents were: (46.7%) for large scale of killings, (16.3%) for human rights abuses by security forces and 15.3 per cent respondents have joined protest rallies for Kashmir freedom movement. However 48.3 per cent respondents said that they have registered their protests against what they see as human rights abuses through the Social networking sites like Facebook, Tweeter etc.

Table 6.8: Description of the Youth who Believe that Violence can Only Bring Change and Participate in Violence and Strikes

Belief in Violence/Strike activities	*Great extent*	*Somewhat*	*Not at all*	*No opinion*
A Political Strike	511	252	103	112
B General Strike	523	290	83	94
C Religious Strike	270	211	209	200
D Student Strike	315	183	423	79
E Social Issues Strike	369	324	177	130
F Strike against Administration	296	198	322	184

Source: Field Study.

The findings also revealed that, a vast majority of respondents i.e. 86.3 per cent have never voted in their life time. They were of the opinion that they are disappointed with Government. Majority of the respondents' i.e. 89.3 per cent identified unemployment as one of the main problems facing by the youth and 71.3 per cent respondents felt that they are confronted with corruption each and every time." Corruption appears to be a major factor affecting the administrative and regulatory environment in Kashmir. Corruption perversely aggravates delays and inefficiencies. Facing corruption is also often a traumatic experience, added the respondents. About 35.1 per cent respondents felt that drug addiction is emerging as a major problem that has taken the youth of valley in its grip.

Finally, majority of the 96 per cent respondents placed peace/conflict resolution at the very top list of priorities. The respondents felt that peace is something more important than most other issues but it has to be just peace, not just the shunning of violence. If the Kashmir problem is not resolved, it would remain burden for future generations. Kashmir issue has to be solved once for all in a just manner. Almost 89 per cent respondents were principally concerned about their physical security. The presence of a huge security and easy availability of arms are two major factors that have direct bearing on security issues. Around 69 per cent respondents gave priority to employment after peace and security. Better employment opportunities would reduce trauma opined the respondents. More than 63 per cent respondents were concerned about their education. The respondents viewed education the passport to a better future. The respondents believe that education is essential to their survival, protection and full recovery from their experience of conflict.

Tourism, Sports and Youth

The Valley of Kashmir known for its natural beauty throughout the world witnesses heavy flow of tourists every year. It is a very important employment sector. In 1997 the Hotel, Catering and Tourism (HCT) sector employed more than 10 per cent of the workforce worldwide (ILO, 2000). Many developing countries depend, to a great extent, economically on this industry. Tourism comprises a broad range of occupations and workplaces. On one side it covers luxury hotels and government restaurants in the formal sector, on the other side cheap boarding houses and road-side food-stalls are found in the informal sector. Tourism and services is one of the four main sectors where youth are working. Business activity has increased in this sector in the past. It is mainly located in the north, south and central Kashmir areas, which are the preferred areas of tourists that visit the naturally bound beautiful valley. Tourist facilities are diverse in these areas. In the inland, mountains and Savannas areas, located inland, attract tourist for safaris. Many youth are working in inland tourist areas,

Table 6.9: Description of Youth about Panchayat System in Kashmir

Statements	*Agree*		*Disagree*		*No opinion*
	Strongly agree	*Somewhat agree*	*Strongly disagreed*	*Somewhat disagree*	
A Panchayats have empowered people	57	98	412	134	299
B Panchayats have resulted in reducing discrimination	35	35	631	110	189
C Panchayats have led to increase in corruption	489	240	70	65	136
D Panchayat system should be eradicated	615	197	67	49	68

Source: Field Study.

Table 6.10: Description of Youth Suggesting Aim/Goal of State Government for Next Decade

Sl. No.	*Aim/Goal*	*Number*	*Percentage*
1.	Guaranteeing secure employment for all youth in Kashmir	843	84.3
2.	Betterment of health services	645	64.5
3.	Stop violence against youth	765	76.5
4.	Providing good education facilities	598	59.8
5.	Conflict resolution	960	96.0
6.	Infrastructure Development	487	48.7

Source: Field Study.

and in nearby hotels and restaurants. Job security is poor for youth in the tourism industry of Kashmir. The tourism sector in Kashmir is totally dependent on customer flows from outside. The amount of tourists varies between seasons and is very much dependent on external factors, such as weather conditions or the economies of the tourists' origin. The disturbance in the state from last two decades has aggravated and worsened the tourist inflow to the state which has resulted into deteriorating condition of tourist based economy of the people. Lack of tourists makes the youth face lack of jobs and consequently money to support their family or pay or their own education.

Two and a half decades conflict has severely hurt the sports sector of the valley. Sports lover youth of the valley are struggling to save their lives from violent armed conflict. The sports infrastructure in the valley is badly hit during the violent turmoil period. In such a situation the deep naturally constructed relationship between youth and sports was lost to a great extent. To rebuild the lost relationship between sports and youth strong efforts have been made which resulted in great success as we experience it from a decade now. Many young players in different sports categories have reached to national level squads and are now representing India in different competitions at the international level. From cricket which is the most popular game in the valley of Kashmir; football, hockey, volleyball, table-tennis, badminton and other games are being played across the length and breadth of valley in contemporary times. But unemployment, socio-psychological problems and other security related issues in different areas are stopping youth from participating fully in different sports activities. State government has taken a number of steps from last ten to fifteen years for restoring the sports activities in the state especially in the valley of Kashmir and has taken adequate steps to upgrade the inadequate infrastructure for giving boost to the different sports activities in the State. Every effort is being made by the State to involve and divert youth towards sports activities for keeping them out from getting infected with anti-establishment and anti-State activities. Sports character is also taken up by experts as an important step to safeguard young population of the State from socio-psychological impacts of disastrous violent conflict in the valley of Kashmir from last two and a half decades.

Youth, State and Governance

Governance is a notoriously difficult term to engage. In part, this is because it encompasses a subject matter which is too vast to be dealt by a single individual. Indeed, it requires a team work drawn from different disciplines. To be sure, governance is a dynamic concept; it is in flux, it changes, modifies and adapts itself with the changing times in the enabling environment of nexus between knowledge and power. The defining feature of the progress and growth of human civilization is, in the words of Toynbee, "progress towards self-determination"—the capacity of the civilization to understand the challenges and its capacity to respond creatively by constantly making amendments, modifications and even radical changes in the existing systems, institutions and techniques.[1] However, as articulated by Foucault, the knowledge must have the backing of the dominant discourse of the time, and its exponents should have more power than its critics for making the knowledge popular and respectable. This is exactly true to the emergence of 'New Governance' discourse. Clearly, the existing patterns of governance were flawed, but it is a fact that the fundamental reason for the New Governance to become a 'universal truth' is that it is the 'ideological product' of the hegemonic power and its controlled global institutions—World Bank, International Monetary Fund (IMF), World Trade Organization (WTO), Asian Development Bank, Organs of United Nations like United Nations Development Programme (UNDP), Organization of Economic Development and Co-operation (OECD) and others—international mechanisms and multilateral and bilateral agreements. What is more important is the fact that since the new governance is seen as the historic ascendance of an ever-evolving concept for thinking about the good of the mankind, the donor institutions and the aid giving countries made the adoption of the parameters of new governance as the basic conditionality for qualifying to receive loan, assistance and aid besides earning a place of respectability in the comity of nations. Both for dependency reasons as well as for the fact that the parameters appear relatively plausible albeit on a dominant-marginal spectrum, the new governance became the global governance ethic—the mirrors through which governments of all the countries see their self-image and reach self-appraisals.

Governance is both a cause and effect. While it impacts every structure of the society, it is itself the product of its own specific context or, to be more accurate, contexts. Context matters to regional governance in two different ways. It is important in the sense that most of the explanatory factors that are causally related to governance are regional in origin, and their effectiveness is determined by the will and capacity of the dominant and the alternative discourses of the region to intersect, contradict, destabilize, cancel or modify each other. Since governance is the complex and the interconnected nature of a very multifaceted combination of factors, and as contextual diversity rules at the heart of Indian nation with each region and sub-region having its own history, packages of historical legacies and political memories, political geography, historical evolution and social, cultural, economic and ideological conditions, specific relations with the center, institutional arrangements, elite initiatives, pressures generated from below, relative strength, diversity and aspirations of the stake holders of regional politics and so on, it is not difficult to see different regions/states experiencing the problem of governance in different ways. Even other changes which cascade down from the apex of the national political system or from beyond the national frontiers also vary from region to region.

Since there can be no single definition of governance due to varied contexts and differences between different countries and regions, the term governance in this work is used as a general concept to describe the pattern of rule with emphasis on democracy and public policy. However, to avoid confusion the term 'New Governance' is used to refer to those broad parameters which after the 1980s are generally accepted as important for fulfilling the aspirations for a better world. In terms of contextual variations governance in Kashmir can be broadly divided into the following phases: 1947–1953, 1953–1963, 1963–1975, 1975–1989, 1990–1996, 1996–2001 and 2001-2 till date, each with its own specific characteristics.[2] During the phase I, the governance was influenced and impacted by the internationalization of Kashmir dispute. Instrument of Accession, Accession dispute, economic crisis caused by the rupture of commercial ties following the Accession, Naya Kashmir Manifesto, Jacobian ideology of NC,[3] Shaikh Abdullah's emotional commitment with the special position of Kashmir, activities of divisive forces operating at regional and State level and integrationist moves of the Centre. The second phase can be called as governance for integration through coercion and consent. Thus on the one hand we see Article 370 being eroded and the anti-integrationist forces being ruthlessly suppressed and democracy ruled out for Kashmir, we at the same see the governments busy in manufacturing consent through development, populist measures, soft budget constraints, corruption, propaganda and entertainment. The third phase was also informed by the policy to strengthened Kashmir's integration with India but the strategy changed from coercion to limited liberalization underlined by civil liberties and decentralization; from rampant corruption to checking misuse of power; and from promoting a small section of influential population for forging alliances with the creamy layers to promoting the interests of the society, especially the poor section of the society to satisfy the quest of bridging gulf between rich and poor. However the policy of eroding the Article 370 which began during the second phase reached to its climax besides the continuation of farce elections, populist policies, promotion of public sector, and soft budget constraints. The fourth phase is characterized by two new developments: (1) semi-democracy in that though the governments were based on the popular vote, they were intolerant towards opposition; (2) semi-good governance because though the governments completed the agenda of abolishing feudalism initiated immediately after independence, cancelled subsidies on ration, introduced the single line administration, created new districts, stepped up developmental schemes, initiated the process of saving huge losses by converting some public undertakings into corporations and institutionalized the recruitment system for sub-ordinate services, nevertheless misuse of power, patrimonial role of the State, huge gap between income and expenditure, unemployment, deficit of some basic facilities like electricity, hospitals, roads and drinking water continued to stay as grave problems. The governance during the 1990 – 1996 was appropriated by maintaining law and order disrupted by mass based militancy necessitating the imposition of governor's rule and the imposition of draconian laws which perhaps resulted into the violation of human rights. This phase also witnessed the intensification of ethno-regional aspirations by the Jammu Hindu Dogras and Buddhists of Leh against what they called their domination by Kashmiris and discriminatory attitude against them. The phase V saw the beginning towards revival of democratic government within the constraints of deficit of peace which made the government notorious for promoting counter insurgents and the resultant violation of human rights. This phase is however, marked by an initiative to respond the current discourse on governance as is evident by the appointment of by such committee as the Committee on Economic Reforms and the State Autonomy Committee. The current phase from 2001 onwards is underlined by some significant changes both to achieve peace as well as to respond the modern discourse/s on governance within the peculiar political, geo-political, economic and cultural conditions of Kashmir.[4] However, the challenges are too varied and too serious to be solved without responding to them creatively rather than copying the policies from unequal comparisons.

Perhaps no other factor has been so overarching in shaping the governance in Kashmir as is the political instability which constitutes the defining feature of the post-1947 history of Kashmir. The dispute on Kashmir and the dispute among the regions have been creating permanent instability in Kashmir. The ultimate result of the uncertainty was that the politics of Jammu and Kashmir revolving around personalities was always focused on creating peace and stability in the state even at the cost of good governance. Economically also the State suffered heavily right from the time of British colonialism. The partition of India and the Indo-Pak dispute over Kashmir gave last blow to shatter the ramshackle economic structure of the state. The fact that the Centre always remained concerned with bringing stability within the State giving a free hand to the successive State governments led to growth of corruption, nepotism and favouritism in the State.

Since in J&K the parties in power owed their position not to popular vote but to manipulations and fraud committed with the willing as well as forced cooperation of the bureaucracy one could only expect an unholy alliance between the ruling class and the bureaucracy to grossly misuse power to serve their personal interests at the altar of justice, fair play and societal interests. This is what exactly happened. Not surprisingly, therefore, in the State of Jammu and Kashmir it seems following a mirage to expect getting ones due if one does not have any one to do *siffarish* – to recommend, to push either in lieu of bribe (*rishwat*) or through the route of some proximity (*rishta, jan-pehchan*). In fact *rishwat* and *siffarish* have been the only two effective qualifications to aspire for a government job, promotion, 'prize' posting, convenient posting, contract, subsidy, loan, movement of file, a favourable note on the file, redress of a genuine demand, punishment to criminal and justice to innocent. If one possesses these two 'qualifications' impossible could become possible, and if not then the vice versa. This had an adverse impact on the aspiring youth of Kashmir whose number was growing with time. The result was that the "State machinery lost its credibility, justice became a causality, corruption made deeper inroads, productivity of the administration declined, regional and ethnic loyalties deepened and groupism, factionalism, rivalry, undercutting, intrigue and competition to excel in maneuvering became the hall mark of administration".[5] There are hundreds of cases of gross violation of rules, corruption and nepotism during the successive regimes of the State. Interestingly, the commissions of inquiry were constituted almost all the governments related to cases of corruption and misuse of authority.

In the statutory public undertakings, the influential persons grossly misused their position. For example in the State Financial Corporation four sons of political elements were appointed.[6] It was also a routine matter to appoint to the subordinate services especially Class IV and daily wagers only, what the ruling political party called their 'workers' – those who actively supported it in winning elections – to the complete exclusion of their opponents. The ex-Governor of Kashmir, Jagmohan says that 'In February 1988 I found that in the preceding nine months over Rupees three crore had been spent on employing daily wagers at the instance of the Ministers'.[7]

It was during the Governor's rule that a major reform was carried out by promulgating the Jammu and Kashmir State Subordinate Services Recruitment Act, 1986 which provided for the establishment of an independent statutory Subordinate Service Selection Board. But the tradition of manipulation and nepotism was so strongly ingrained in Kashmir's political system that as soon as Dr. Farooq Abdullah came back to power in November, 1986 his government proceeded to repeal this Act. One may not approve the imposition of Governor's rule, the fact remains that political interference in the delivery of justice was considerably minimized during the period. And once the 'elected' government came to power, the old game of manipulation of personal party patronage resumed with full vigor. An example will suffice. During the coalition government of NC and the Congress, 1,100 posts were created in Agriculture Department in mid-1989. In regard to filling of these posts, a dispute arose between the coalition partners – whether the posts would be divided between the NC and Congress in the ratio of 80:20 or 70:30 or 60:40.[8] This was the situation in 1989 when the militancy had already started knocking at the door of the State Government.

The post 1989-90 saw the emergence of entirely new problems besides further deepening the crisis in the already existing infirmities. The new problems that arose with no precedent are the emergence of radical politics posing a serious challenge to the state, and the resultant violation of human rights. The curbing of militancy and the restoration of peace took precedence over all other fundamental issues which a government is supposed to attend in normal times albeit with the passage of time it was realized that military option has to be accompanied by *good governance* to wean away youth from radical politics. It was in this context that since 2002 good governance became the mantra for all governments starting with Peoples Democratic Party's (PDP) policy of *Healing Touch Policy*. Along with other measures taken by the PDP led coalition government, headed by Mufti Mohammad Syed, a very significant development that took place during the Mufti government was the employment of a large chunk of un-employed youth. There is no doubt that one of the important factors that made militancy mass movement in 1989-90 was the problem of unemployment as we find a good number of youths joining it either with the hope of qualifying themselves for an appointment in the state services in the perceived not-distant 'Azad Kashmir'[9], or to give an outlet to their frustration or improve their position by wielding power through the barrel of gun or settling scores with their exploiters.[10] The problem of unemployment is also fraught with serious consequences of keeping the pot of militancy boiling for the same reasons which attracted hoards of people to join it at the time of its introduction. Therefore, it has been the policy of the government to give employment to as many people as possible in the absence of any private sector worth the name. During the NC regime the emphasis was laid on recruiting youths in police force to kill two birds with one stone; yet under the pressure of financial crisis and the inflated service sector, recruitment in government jobs, except for a few posts referred to Public Service Commission and SSRB, was banned under the orders of the central government. As a part of its policy to heal the wounds of the people and restore peace by weaning the people away from militancy, the Mufti government insisted on the central government to lift the ban on recruitments and provide special employment packages. The ban was not only lifted, but the Prime Minister gave two packages in 4 months, providing one lakh jobs in two years.[11] About 30 thousand qualified youths were appointed as *Rahbar-i-Taleem* teachers; 2000 educated youth were appointed on contractual basis in agriculture, medical, Engineering, and Physical Education departments; self-help groups of 2000 jobless engineers were set up and they were provided Rs. 4.20 crores; 15,000 were absorbed in 7500 anganwadi centers; 7000 in Home and 2000 were recruited in J&K Police.[12] It was also towards the end of the Mufti government that all the departments were directed to refer the vacant positions to SSRB and Public Service Commission. As a result hundreds of posts were subsequently advertised by the above recruiting agencies. Besides providing employment to large numbers, which in itself is a great achievement especially in the context of Kashmir where neutralizing discontentment is of crucial significance, what is more important, is that to a large extent these posts were filled up on transparent basis.[13]

The Mufti government also took steps for promoting investor-friendly industrial policy to attract private sector involvement of bringing about world class infrastructural development, industrialization of the backward blocks of the state and modernization of the existing units. In order to encourage investment in the State, the Chief Minister went all over the country. He even went to London, sent a team to Malaysia and another one to Dubai.[14] It generated a wide response. Several big industrial houses showed keen interest to invest in the State. By the mid June 2004 the government had already received investment proposals of over Rs. 1200 crore with an employment potential for 6000[15]. Forty projects had come up at Samba and Bari Brahmna Industrial Estates.[16]

To facilitate entrepreneurs, the government developed industrial estates in all the districts. A number of industrial estates were developed in and around Jammu city and around Srinagar city in the Kashmir Valley for ready allotment of industrial plots to the promoters. Further, a Growth Centre at a cost of Rs. 30 crore was developed at Samba, 40 km from Jammu on the National Highway towards Pathankot. Another growth centre was taken up for implementation at Lassipora, Pulwama, about 40 km from Srinagar in the Kashmir Valley. In addition, an Export Promotion Industrial Park (EPIP) was planned near the Srinagar airport. A Software Technology Park (STP) was also technically cleared for development in the existing Rangreth.[17] To motivate more and more industrial houses to invest in the state, the government announced a new industrial policy (NIP) in January 2004.[18] Besides this steps were taken to promote horticulture, agricultural sector and to promote self-employment.

However, the state of J&K continues to face a serious crisis on account of ever growing number of educated unemployed youth. As per the official figures, 5,94,172 youth have been registered at the district level employment exchanges across the state till September 2012. Out of these registered unemployed youth, 3,12,977 were from Kashmir region and 2,81,195 from Jammu division.[19] Although the official website of Jammu and Kashmir Employment Exchange puts figure of registered unemployed youth at 3,07,827 by the end of September 2013,[20] however the officials maintain the actual number of unemployed youth may be much higher as the registration is a voluntary process. To address this problem there is an urgent need to devise a multi-pronged strategy involving public and private players.

Taking a lead in increasing employment opportunities for the youth of the State, the then Chief Minister of the State Mr. Omar Abdullah, in a renewed effort at an award ceremony held in Mumbai in 2009 urged corporate India to engage in imparting skills to the young people in Kashmir to solve two interrelated problems of employment and 'unemployability'.[21] "I am not asking you to look to invest immediately. I am looking to you to help me create the conditions that will make you want to invest in Jammu and Kashmir.... It is the problem of unemployability that corporate India can help me with by helping give youngsters of Jammu and Kashmir a skill-set that will make them attractive not just in the state but in the rest of the country," Omar said.[22] As a result of seriousness shown by the government 18 polytechnics were set up in districts in which none was present hitherto. Aegis, a subsidiary of the ESSAR group, laid the foundation of one of its BPOs at Rangreth, Srinagar, which by 2011 had employed 500 youth.[23] Collaboration with the CII was initiated with the formation of a joint task force with the CM as the Chairman and Sunil Mittal of Bharti Airtel as the co-chairperson. Urging the investors to free their minds of the idea of J&K being a militancy-hit state the Chief Minister urged the corporate sector to invest in farming, power, tourism, IT and handicrafts.[24] Corporate India called for the setting up of development and infrastructure board, universalizing education, and providing skill development in rural areas. As an initiative in Corporate Social Responsibility (CSR) in rural and urban areas, the JK Bank planned to set up 1109 common services centers or *khidmat* centers, which would also generate employment of which the first 300 were inaugurated on February 17, 2010.[25] "The initiative serves two important purposes that people of J&K are in need of. First, it generates employment besides encouraging entrepreneurship. Second, it helps to bring the state on the IT map which is the objective of national e-governance project", said the then Chairman and CE of J&K Bank Dr. Haseeb Drabu.[26]

The State Level Advisory Committee on Youth Programme launched a plan to employ 8000 youth as tourist guides under the PM's package of Rs. 148 crore for the purpose through Nehru Yuva Kendras (youth centres) and was to be implemented by the Jammu and Kashmir Entrepreneurship Development Institute (JKEDI). By September, the JK Bank entered into a partnership with the government to provide 65 per cent of the loan, while 35 per cent of non-refundable seed money would be given by the JKEDI. The scheme provided for non-refundable seed money to the maximum limit of Rs. 3 lakh for undergraduates/graduates, Rs. 5 lakh for post-graduates and Rs. 7.5 lakh for doctors/engineers/and those with MBA degree. An Overseas Employment Corporation was set up in June 2010. Initiatives were also launched to help the small industry to grow and to provide employment to people in the Valley alone. An IT Park is being created in Budgam.[27]

To meet the aspirations of the youth, an Expert Group under the chairmanship of C. Rangarajan was set up in 2010 to enhance employment opportunities in public and private sector.[28] The group submitted its report, which was based on the NSSO data on unemployment in the State in 2007-08 of 1.3 lakh as the baseline and the District Employment and Counseling Centers (DECC) data of 4.48 lakh in November 2009, 5.89 lakh in March 2010 and as the aspirational ceiling number, in February 2011. The focus of the expert group was on human resource development.

The Group devised a Skill, Empowerment and Employment (SEE) initiative in consultation with the Ministry of Human Resource Development. This initiative seeks to train 50,000 to 1 lakh youth in three to five years. Due to its experience in these matters, Ministry of Rural Development (MoRD) was made the implementing agency. The scheme will be aimed at moving the youth from the unorganized to the organized sector. The funding for the scheme would come from two sources and be managed under two windows. The first window will be for training the rural BPL youth for which, 75 per cent of the funding will come from Ministry of Rural Development (MoRD) under the Sampoorna Gram Swarozgar Yojana (SGSY), while for the remaining 25 per cent a special allocation can be made under PM's J&K Package to the Ministry of Home Affairs (MHA) who can then partner MoRD in implementing the scheme. The second window will be for rural non- BPL and urban youth for which, 100 per cent of the funding will be under the PM's J&K package to be placed with the MHA. To engage the youth, another initiative suggested was to identify 10-20 companies across industry sectors to collaborate with an educational institution and run special training programs to enhance employability for 8000 students per year over a five year period. This would translate into 40,000 youth in J&K becoming employable in various sectors across India.

The Prime Minister's Employment Guarantee Programme (PMEGP), a centrally sponsored credit linked subsidy scheme envisages the generation of employment opportunities through establishment of micro enterprises in rural as well as urban areas. The scheme has a total outlay of more than Rs. 4000 crores, and has been working very well in J&K for the past number of years. In 2009-10 the State set up 1782 units at an expenditure of Rs. 18.2 crores while in 2010-11, 1036 units have already been set up at an expenditure of Rs. 19 crores. This scheme also has a component for skill development to build capacities of the rural artisans. The Expert Group recommended an allocation of Rs. 10 crores for this component over the next four years.

Around three lakh youth were given voluntary service allowance under the Sheri-e-Kashmir Employment and Welfare Programme for Youth (SKEWPY) launched on 5th December 2009. In order to help them explore new avenues of self-employment and encourage young entrepreneurs to become partners of self and state. Under the centrally sponsored scheme 'HIMAYAT' one lakh matriculate and higher qualification youth will be targeted for training in various fields to prepare them for the job market. The programme was officially launched with the handing over of placement offer letters to 1060 trainees in Srinagar in 2011 by Shri Jairam Ramesh Minister of Rural Development, Government of India, Mr. Omar Abdullah, Chief Minister of Jammu and Kashmir, and Dr. C. Rangarajan, Chairman Economic Advisory Council to Prime Minister of

India.[29] Similarly under the 'UDAAN' scheme 40,000 technically qualified graduates and Post-Graduates will be trained for employment in large industrial houses all over India in five years.

However, it needs to be stressed that the State is yet to evolve a comprehensive policy for purposeful engagement of youth in governance. The state is fast moving towards hundred per cent literacy and the number of unemployed educated youth is posing a serious challenge. In the absence of private sector and limited capacity of the State sector to accommodate this growing number the State is moving towards a dangerous situation. The policies started by governments in recent times prove half-way house as these policies don't provide attractive incentives for the youth.

Notes

1. Toynbee, Arnold, *A Study of History*, D.C. Somervell (ed.), Abridgement, Vol. 3, Oxford University Press, New York & London, 1947.
2. Wani Aijaz Ashraf, *Governance in Kashmir Since 1947*, Ph.D Thesis (unpublished), Department of political Science, University of Kashmir, 2014.
3. Bose Summantra, *Kashmir: Roots of Conflict, Paths to Peace,* 2003, p. 27.
4. Wani Aijaz Ashraf, *Ibid.*
5. Jagmohan, *My Frozen Turbulence in Kashmir*, Chapter, Roots: Hidden Veins.
6. Governor Jagmohan's note to the State Cabinet sent on August, 7, 1987. The note has been reproduced by him in his book, *My Frozen Turbulence in Kashmir,* p. 192.
7. *Ibid.*, p. 199.
8. *Ibid.*, p. 198.
9. Local Informants.
10. After verifying the background of the common militants and examining the economic stratification of the society together with corruption, nepotism and growing levels of consciousness on account of educational development and exposure through mass media, it becomes quite clear that the large number of people joined militancy for economic considerations. This is precisely the reason why immediately after it started, the militancy began to peter out as the economic driven militancy could not withstand the counter

insurgency pressures. Not only this, they also derailed the movement by using gun for serving their economic interests. And ultimately the militancy became the exclusive provenance of those elements who were ideologically motivated, especially the religious oriented ideology.

11. Department of Information, Government of Jammu and Kashmir, *Kashmir Times*, November, 02, 2003.
12. *Ibid.*
13. This is especially true of *Rahbar-i-Taleem* teachers.
14. Chief Minister Mufti Mohammad Sayeed in an interview with T. Ghosh, For details see *Jammu and Kashmir Turning a New Page*, Published by Department of Information, Government of Jammu and Kashmir, 2004, pp. 8-10.
15. Department of Industries, Government of Jammu and Kashmir
16. *Ibid.*
17. *Jammu and Kashmir Turning a New Page, op. cit.*, p. 33.
18. *New Industrial Policy 2004 and Package of incentives for development of Industries* in J&K came into force by Government Order No. 21-Ind. Of 2004, Dated: 27-01-2004., in reference to Cabinet Decision No. 191/1, Dated: 23-01-2004.
19. http://www.greaterkashmir.com/news/2013/Mar/10/jk-has-highest-unemployment-rate-in- north- india-42.asp Accessed on January 23, 2014.
20. http://jakemp.nic.in/aboutus/qualification%20wise%20Breakup.htm Accessed on January 23, 2014.
21. Outlook, "Give J&K a Chance-Omar tells India Inc", http://news.outlookindia.com/items. aspx?artid=651969 Accessed on January 23, 2014.
22. *Ibid.*
23. Anant Arpita, *Beyond Stereotypes: Contours of the Transition in Jammu and Kashmir, op. cit.*, pp. 77-78.
24. *Daily Excelsior*, June 16, 2009, http://www.ipcs.org/news/jammu-kashmir/omar-seeks-investment-in-jk-by-private-companies-2925.html Accessed on January 23, 2014.
25. *Greater Kashmir*, February 17, 2014, http://www.ipcs.org/news/jammu-kashmir/omar-seeks-investment-in-jk-by-private-companies-2925.html Accessed on January 23, 2014.
26. *Ibid.*
27. Anant Arpita, *Beyond Stereotypes: Contours of the Transition in Jammu and Kashmir, Op. cit.*
28. The other members were N.R. Narayan Murthy, Tarun Das, T. Nand Kumar, Shakeel Qalander, Y.V. Sharma, Bharat Vyas, Sanjay Mitra and K. Skandan.
29. Government of Jammu and Kashmir; *Three years of People's Friendly Government*, p. 7.

7
Conclusion and Policy Implications

The study underscores the fact that youth face numerous challenges while making the transition to adulthood. These challenges call for programme interventions at the youth, family and service delivery levels. Key programme recommendations emerging from this study are highlighted below. The following suggestions and recommendations could help in overcoming the youth issues in Kashmir in general and affected and vulnerable youth in particular:

- Activities must address school-level barriers, notably, poor infrastructure, quality of education and academic failure. There is a need to incorporate livelihood skills building models within the school setting that will not only raise young people's aspirations regarding their education and careers but also provide them opportunities to gain market-driven job skills. There is also a need to focus on providing better training and ensuring accountability for teachers—investments that are likely to improve the quality of schooling experiences for youth. Efforts need to be made to adjust school timings, including the establishment of evening schools to enable children and youth to accommodate work or business without sacrificing their education especially higher studies. The study further reveals that several sub-groups of youth—young women, the married, the rural, those belonging to poor households and those belonging to lower castes and groups—remain considerably disadvantaged call for efforts that specifically target these vulnerable groups. Interventions are needed that give youth who missed the opportunity to obtain adequate formal education a second chance to acquire equivalency to formal education.

- The Problem of health and education are the key areas of attention. Youth and especially students yearn for greater exposure, facilities, counselling, accountability and promotion of creativity. The reconstruction of the social infrastructure (education, health) must be recovered for future perspectives of youth. The government as well as non-governmental agencies and organisation can provide valuable help in this regard.
- Large numbers of innocent children are forced to work in different sectors of the economy due to the poor family conditions and there is a special need to provide conditional grants and targeted subsidies to these disadvantaged groups, which would encourage parents to opt for schooling over work for their children. At the same time, it is important to vigorously enforce existing laws that prohibit child labour. Both administration as well as civil society must be mobilized to ensure that irrespective of caste, class, gender, residence, etc. all children are enrolled in school for quality education.
- This research points to the effective un-employability of significant proportions of youth. It is notable that while considerable proportions of urban youth reported exposure to computer skills, English language skills and so on, rural youth tended to opt for relatively traditional vocational skills and may not have had the opportunity to learn about market needs or develop appropriate skills for which a demand exists. It is also notable that those who were engaged in economic activity were working largely as semiskilled, unskilled or sometimes as skilled non-agricultural labourers.

Moreover, considerable proportions of youth, particularly, the educated were unemployed, suggesting a possible disconnect between youth skills and market needs.

- It has been seen that Youth living in conflict situation are highly prone to psychosocial troubles. Therefore a strong community based psycho-social support mechanism is highly required to address the needs of youth especially who have been directly affected. In addition to it, the existing institutions or establishments in this regard needs further strengthening.
- There is a need to initiate schemes to assist victims of armed conflict especially the youth-headed households. There is need to improve the situation of youth by strengthening their capacities and to increase the quality and quantity of opportunities available to young people for full, effective and constructive participation in society.
- The state and government must significantly strengthen investments in programmes that enable youth to make a successful transition to work roles. Enhancing employability would depend to a considerable extent on the improvements in educational attainment; it would also require greater investment in enabling youth to acquire vocational skills. Formal mechanisms must be developed that provide opportunities to youth to acquire skills for which there is an established demand, and that link eligible youth to market opportunities. At the same time, efforts are needed to promote self-employment and entrepreneurship through various livelihood schemes, for example, providing soft loans to youth to enable them to set up their own business enterprises like the scheme introduced under Sheri Kashmir Employment Guarantee Scheme. Also required are efforts to evaluate existing programmes aimed at job creation to assess their reach and impact in enabling young people to make a successful transition to work roles, upscale successful models, raise awareness

among youth about their availability and ensure that these programmes do indeed reach young people.

- There is need of avenues for youth to participate in social and cultural events like festivals, dramas, traditions, music, which shall be helpful for distressed youth.
- It has been seen that conflict has changed the socialization patterns of youth. The family structure which is based on love and affection has been broken. Family reunification is an urgent need. For the proper growth and development, Youth must live in safe environment, provided by family. Parents have a big role to play for providing proper socialization to youth so that the impact is visible at the family level to community level and to society as a whole.
- Youth participation should be encouraged at all levels of social interaction, from the neighbourhood, school, and local community to the national and international levels in a multi-track diplomacy approach. They should be given responsibilities according to their capacities and be taken seriously.
- The study highlights the limited agency of young women and the persistence of gender double standards among youth. Young women were particularly disadvantaged in terms of school enrolment, participation in wage earning activities, and exposure to mass media. While young women were as likely as young men to have participated in vocational training programmes, most young women had undergone training in traditional skills, such as tailoring and handicrafts. Socialization was gendered and parental control over their adolescent children's mobility and interactions with peers was stricter for young women than men. Additionally, compared to young men, young women reported less mobility, opportunities to build peer networks, decision-making authority in matters relating to their own lives and control over resources. And although young women were more

likely than young men to express equitable gender role attitudes. These findings call for attention to promote life skills education programmes for young women, both unmarried and married, that will not only raise their awareness of new ideas and the world around them but also enable them to put new information into practice, encourage them to question gender stereotypes, develop self-esteem and strengthen their skills in problem-solving, decision-making, communication and inter-personal relations and negotiation. Equally important is to identify safe spaces in which young women can build social networks and find social support among peers. Promoting gender equitable norms and practices requires active engagement with the community. It is essential that programmes for youth work with key community members, such as parents and political and religious leaders in the community, to critically examine prevailing gender norms and forces that perpetuate such norms. Findings suggest that while young women were more likely than young men to report savings, they were somewhat less likely to own a savings account, and, among those who did own an account, considerably less likely to operate the account independently. At the same time, few youth owned a bank or post office account. Programmes are needed that inculcate a savings orientation among young people, that offer savings products that are attractive and appropriate to the small and erratic savings patterns of young people and that enable young women in particular to overcome obstacles related to owning and controlling saving products.

- There is also need to scale up investments in youth to create verifiable indicators for the priority areas and to ensure vulnerable or disadvantaged young people receive special attention. It is necessary to avoid generating false expectations that the situation of youth is going to be vastly improved by means of development programmes alone. In place of ad hoc and small level interventions with grand ambitions, there is need for holistic and crosscutting programmes that reflects the importance of taking into account the necessity of working at multiple levels of society (individual, households, communities) and links programmes that directly target youth with those that benefit youth indirectly. Furthermore, the new programmes must place more emphasis on the social and economic challenges that youth face, rather than assuming that young people are themselves the problem. The new programmes must take into account the necessity for location specific implementation. In the preparatory stages, needs assessments should be situation-based, age-specific and participatory, and should investigate the resourcefulness of young people.

- There is an urgent need to establish safe, well-publicized and confidential mechanism for young women and men to report violence, harassment, and exploitation. Ensure prompt investigation, support for and protection of Youth.
- Majority of youth in valley hold secular attitudes with regard to mixing with a person from another caste and religion, and few engage in community-level violence. Nevertheless, not all youth expressed secular attitudes. Moreover, considerable proportions of youth were dissatisfied with the political process. Finally, relatively few had taken part in civil society, that is, government- or NGO-sponsored programmes or community-led activities. Programmes are needed at the school, college and community levels—through various service programmes, sports and other non-formal mechanisms—that encourage civic participation, incorporate value building components and reinforce secular attitudes and values that espouse responsible citizenship. It is also emphasized that the political system in the state needs to make special efforts to address the concerns of youth and encourage youth

participation in the political processes in more meaningful ways.

- There is also need to amend untrue history versions related with Kashmir problem so that negative stereotypes may diminish. Youth need to be listened to – feel like their views are respected. There is need of Youth councils, NGOs, forums and youth networks. There is need to establish well governed political institutions by giving greater representation and power-sharing to youth, reserving seats for disadvantaged groups, ensuring free and fair elections, and strengthening minority/majority rights (freedom of practice in social, cultural and religious spheres).
- Corruption has been almost institutionalised in government departments and the government is unable to curb it. Nepotism is particularly common. There must be complete accountability and transparency in government and other institutions, and corruption must be stamped out completely. However, we must be primarily accountable to ourselves; people at every level must take a strong stand against corruption.
- Youth Study findings provide considerable evidence suggesting that family life or sex education is urgently needed for youth, both for those in school and those who have discontinued their education. Misconceptions abound on most topics: sex, contraceptive methods including condoms. Where awareness of sexual and reproductive health matters exists, it is superficial in many cases. What is needed is a strong commitment to ensuring that programmes do indeed reach young people, both those in school and out-of-school, married and unmarried, and rural and urban. These programmes should be age-appropriate. Indeed, findings indicate that one in three young women and one in five young men who had received formal family life or sex education reported feeling uncomfortable or embarrassed in the course of

receiving this information, raising questions about the extent to which youth were indeed able to participate freely in discussions and clarify their doubts. It is important that teachers, health care providers and other experts undergo training that enables them to overcome their reluctance to communicate with youth on sensitive sexual and reproductive matters, dispels their misconceptions on these matters. Also needed are efforts to engage parents—providing them with accurate information and working with them to overcome inhibitions about imparting this information to their children, particularly their daughters. Efforts are also needed to inform married young women of their rights so that they have the opportunity to exercise control over their own lives; at the same time, efforts must be made to promote new concepts of masculinity and femininity and egalitarian couple relations among young men and women. While wide gender disparities place young women at a notable disadvantage, Youth Study findings highlight that young men are also disadvantaged in many ways. Although socialized with more freedom than their sisters, communication with parents was limited among young men and many did not have decision-making authority in matters pertaining to their life or control over economic resources. Moreover, many were exposed to tobacco products and alcohol, and notable number had married in adolescence. Findings highlight the limited interaction and social distance between parents and young people while growing up and the gendered nature of socialization experiences. Efforts must be made to create a supportive environment for young people. Encourage greater openness and interaction between parents and children, and enable the adoption of gender-egalitarian child-rearing practices. Programmes that aim to encourage universal education must, likewise, address parental concerns about the potential consequences of keeping daughters in school or delaying their marriage.

- Forums and institutions, giving more space to youth, must be established. Platforms such as student unions must be encouraged, so that youth can voice their concerns.
- Youth have a wide range of needs as they prepare for adult roles. They need to develop skills for economic self-reliance. They need citizenship skills, such as teamwork, leadership, the emphasis should be on social integration and meeting the needs of all youth, since the effects of conflict spare none.
- There is a need of adults in taking care of the issues and problems youth in Kashmir are engulfed in. Mentoring of youth by responsible adults in the community helps youth widen their horizons and build pathways toward the future.
- The research divulges symptoms or behaviours suggestive of mental health disorders suggest that there is a need to establish systems that address young people's mental health. Efforts are needed to screen young people for possible mental health disorders when they avail of other primary health services, including, for example, sexual and reproductive health services, and to refer youth with such symptoms to appropriate health facilities and providers. Findings indicate that substantial proportions of young men reported the consumption of tobacco and alcohol. Efforts are needed to sensitize young men about the adverse effects of substance abuse.

This study provides a broad picture of youth in Kashmir. At the same time, findings have raised a number of issues that require further investigation, particularly with regard to the determinants and consequences of youth behaviours and practices during the transition to adulthood in a conflict violence hit valley. Youth Study highlight the need for further research in terms of formative research that explores in greater depth factors impeding successful transitions to adulthood, including enrolment in school and school completion, entry into the labour force, initiation of sexual activity, and marriage and parenthood. Research is also needed that explores the role of peers and the media, socialization practices, young people's access to information and services, and the ways in which these factors contribute to or impede young people's ability to make successful transitions. A better understanding is required moreover of the factors underlying young people's agency and the expression of unequal and equal gender role attitudes. Also required are efforts to refine measures of agency as applicable to young men and women.

A general research recommendation is the urgent need for prospective or panel study designs that follow a cohort of adolescents at regular intervals up to age 35. Prospective study designs would enable researchers to take a life course approach, identify, with compelling data, the factors responsible for healthy transitions to adulthood and point to the ways in which the situation and experiences of youth in adolescence influence their life course at later ages especially in the valley of Kashmir which has experiences heavy loss of life and property and which at the same has impinged mentally the present as they were born when violence was all over in the valley.

Operation research is also needed. While a number of interventions have been initiated in the country intended to address the needs of youth—for example, changing the norms of masculinity and femininity, encouraging education for girls, developing market-based vocational skills and providing family life and sex education—few of these have been rigorously evaluated. Urgently needed, therefore, are carefully designed and rigorously tested intervention models that not only pay attention to the content and delivery of the intervention but also measure effectiveness and acceptability—in short, that will enable a shift from the implementation of *promising* to *best* practices in addressing young people's needs. In order to inform the field, multiple inputs are required. Ultimately, research is needed that monitors the scaling up of successful interventions in terms of their impact on young people's lives and more importantly in the valley of Kashmir.

The Youth Study has documented, the multi-faceted situation of youth in conflict hit Kashmir. The study alerts us to the many challenges confronting youth in Kashmir and their ability to make a successful transition to adulthood. It emphasizes the heterogeneity of youth, not only in terms of their situation but also with regard to their stated needs and preferred mechanisms to address these needs. Programmes must recognize the heterogeneity of young people and interventions and delivery mechanisms should be appropriately tailored to meet their needs. Evidence presented here provides not only a blue-print for the programming needs of youth in Kashmir but also a base-line by which to measure the impact of programmes intended to address youth needs.

Bibliography

Abraham, L. 2001. "Redrawing the *lakshman rekha*: Gender differences and cultural constructions in youth sexuality in urban India," *South Asia*, 24 : 133 56.

Abraham, L. 2002. "*Bhai-behen*, true love, time pass: Friendships and sexual partnerships among youth in an Indian metropolis," *Culture, Health and Sexuality*, 4(3) : 337-53.

Abraham, L. and K.A. Kumar. 1999. "Sexual experiences and their correlates among college students in Mumbai city, India," *International Family Planning Perspectives*, 25(3) : 139-46.

Ahuja, Ram, 1997. *Social Problems in India*. 2nd (ed.) Rawat Publications Jaipur. 193-216.

Alexander, M., L. Garda, S. Kanade *et al.* 2003. *Formation of partnerships among young women and men in Pune district, Maharashtra; Survey Questionnaire,* unpublished. New Delhi: Population Council.

Alexander, M., L. Garda, S. Kanade *et al.* 2006a. *Formation of Partnerships among Young Women and Men in Pune District, Maharashtra*. New Delhi: Population Council.

Alexander, M., L. Garda, S. Kanade *et al.* 2006b. "Romance and sex: Premarital partnership formation among young women and men, Pune district, India," *Reproductive Health Matters* 14(28) : 144-55.

Basu, A.M. 1992. "The status of women and the quality of life among the poor," *Cambridge Journal of Economics*, 16(3) : 249-67.

Bhat, M. Amin and Shazia, *2002,* 'Drug Addiction—A Sociological Study of District Srinagar', cit., in *'Reflections A Compilation of Research studies,'* J&K State Resource Centre University of Kashmir, pp. 173-185.

Bhatia, M.S. and S. Choudhary. 1998. "*Dhat* symptoms: A culture-bound sex neurosis," *Indian Journal of Medical Science* 52 : 30–35.

Bhatia, M.S. and S.C. Malik. 1991. "*Dhat* syndrome: A useful diagnostic entity in Indian culture," *British Journal of Psychiatry* 159 : 691-95.

Bhuiya, I., U. Rob, M.E. Khan *et al.* 2003. "Reproductive health services for adolescents: Recent experiences from a pilot project in Bangladesh," in *Towards Adulthood: Exploring the Sexual and Reproductive Health of Adolescents in South Asia,* eds. S. Bott, S.J. Jejeebhoy, I. Shah *et al.* Geneva: World Health Organisation, pp. 203-6.

Bradford, B., R. Larson and T.S. Saraswathi, 2002. The World's Youth: Adolescence in Eight Regions of the Globe, Cambridge University Press, pp. 4-6.

Chandrashekhar, C.P., J. Ghosh and A. Roychowdhury. 2006. "'The demographic dividend' and young India's economic future," *Economic and Political Weekly,* 41(49) : 5055-63.

Cleland, J. 2001. "Illustrative questionnaire for interview-surveys with young people," in *Asking Young People about Sexual and Reproductive Behaviours: Illustrative Core Instruments,* eds. J. Cleland, R. Ingham and N. Stone. Geneva: World Health Organisation, pp. 5-16.

Dagar, R. 2007. "Rethinking female foeticide: Perspective and issues," in *Sex-selective Abortion in India: Gender, Society and New Reproductive Technologies,* ed. T. Patel. New Delhi: Sage Publications, pp. 91-134.

Demographic Research and Development Foundation Inc. (DRDF) and University of the Philippines Population Institute (UPPI). 2002. *Young Adult Fertility and Sexuality Study [Married Female] Questionnaire.* Quezon City.

Dyson, T. and M Moore. 1983. "On kinship structure, female autonomy, and demographic behaviour in India," *Population and Development Review,* 9(1) : 35–60.

Eisenstadt, S.N.. 1972. *Archetypical Patterns of Youth.* in P.K. Manning and Marcello. T., *Youth and Sociology*, Inc. *cit.*, from Kohli A.S. and Narala. V.; 2004. Youth in Planned Development in India. *Social Change: Issues and Perspectives.* 34(2): 103-104.

Ellickson, P., H. Saner and K.A. McGuigan. 1997. "Profiles of violent youth: Substance use and other concurrent problems," *American Journal of Public Health,* 87 : 985-91.

Gore, M.S., 1977, *Indian Youth, Processes of Socialization,* Vishwa Yuvak Kendra New Delhi, pp. 4-5.

Guttmacher Institute. 2004a. *Ghana National Survey of Adolescents: Survey Questionnaire,* unpublished. New York: Guttmacher Institute.

Hajnal, J. 1953. "Age at marriage and proportion marrying," *Population Studies,* 7(2) : 111–136.

Henrik. 2004. *The Devil in the Demographics: The Effects of Youth Bulges on Domestic Armed Conflict, 1950-2000.*

India Today, Feb 20, 2006, AC-*Nielsen-ORG–MARG,* youth survey, pp. 12 57.

Jejeebhoy, S.J. 2001. "Women's autonomy and reproductive behaviour in India" in *Fertility Transition in South Asia,* eds. Z.A. Sathar and J.F. Phillips. Oxford: Oxford University Press, pp. 221-241.

Jejeebhoy, S.J. and M.P. Sebastian. 2003. "Actions that protect: Promoting sexual and reproductive health and choice among young people in India," *Regional Working Papers, No. 18.* New Delhi: Population Council.

Jejeebhoy, S.J. and M.P. Sebastian. 2004. "Young people's sexual and reproductive health," in *Looking Back, Looking Forward: A Profile of Sexual and Reproductive Health in India,* ed. S.J. Jejeebhoy. New Delhi: Population Council, pp. 138–68.

Joshi, Subhash, 2006, *Children, Youth and Electronic Media: Prospects and* Portents, B.R. Publishing Corporation India, pp. 3-6.

Laird, R.D., G.S. Pettit, K.A. Dodge *et al.* 2003. "Change in parents' monitoring knowledge: Links with parenting, relationship quality, adolescent beliefs, and antisocial behaviour," *Social Development,* 12(3) : 401-19.

Lambert, H. and K. Wood. 2005. "A comparative analysis of communication about sex, health and sexual health in India and South Africa: Implications for HIV prevention," *Culture, Health and Sexuality,* 7(6) : 527-41.

Mallick, Anupriyo, 2007, 'Suicide and Youth: A Case Study of Kolkata', *Social Welfare,* Vol. 54, No. 4, pp. 28-29.

Mannheim, Karal, 1943. *Diagnosis of Our Times,* p. 33, *op. cit.,* in Lakshmi Narayana, H.D., 1985, *College Youth Challenge and Response,* Mittal Publications New Delhi, pp. 3-6.

Mehra, S., R. Savithri and L. Coutinho. 2002. "Sexual behaviour among unmarried adolescents in Delhi, India: Opportunities despite parental controls," Paper presented at the IUSSP Regional Population Conference, Bangkok, June.

Mensch, B.S., D.N. Anh and W.H. Clark. 2000. *Adolescents and Social Change in Vietnam: Preliminary Report.* Hanoi: Population Council and Institute of Sociology.

Merton, R.K, , 1968. pp 185-214 in Yedla, C. Simhadri. 1992. *Global Youth, Peace and Development: The Role of Science and Technology in the Contemporary Society.* Vol. II. Ajanta Publications Delhi, India.

Ministry of Law and Justice. 2009. *The Right of Children to Free and Compulsory Education Act 2009, No. 35 of 2009, The Gazette of India.* New Delhi: Ministry of Law and Justice, Government of India.

Ministry of Youth Affairs and Sports. 2003. *National Youth Policy 2003.* New Delhi: Ministry of Youth Affairs and Sports, Government of India.

Misra, D.K. and M. Jain, 1975, *Youth, University and Community,* New Delhi: S. Chand & Company, p. 9.

Nation Children's Fund (UNICEF). *2005. Adolescence Education: National Framework and State Action Plan (2005-06).* New Delhi: MOHRD, NACO and UNICEF.

National Research Council and Institute of Medicine. 2005. *Growing Up Global: The Changing Transition to Adulthood in Developing Countries.* Washington, DC: National Academies Press.

National Sample Survey Organisation (NSSO). 2006. *Employment and Unemployment Situation in India 2004-05, Part 1, NSS 61st Round.* New Delhi: NSSO, Government of India.

Out Look, The Weekly News Magazine, 27 May - 2 June, 2008, pp. 51-64.

Patel, V. and G. Andrew. 2001. "Gender, sexual abuse and risk behaviours: A survey of school-based adolescents in Goa," *National Medical Journal of India* 14:263–67. Philippines: DRDF and UPPI.

Planning Commission. 2007b. *Poverty Estimates for 2004-05,* Press release, March. New Delhi: Government of India.

Ponsioen, J.A., 1966, *The Situation of Youth in a Changing Society,* Institute of Social Studies, The Hague, p. 9.

Ram, F., R.K. Sinha, S.K. Mohanty *et al.* 2006. *Marriage and Motherhood: An Exploratory Study of the Social and Reproductive Health Status of Married Young Women in Gujarat and West Bengal, India.* New Delhi: Population Council.

Reddy, M.V. and C.R. Chandrashekar. 1998. "Prevalence of mental and behavioural disorders in India: a meta-analysis," *Indian Journal of Psychiatry,* 40(2):149 57.

Royse, S. and Celia Verghese, July 2007, *Social Welfare,* vol. 54, No. 4, pp. 33 36.

Sachdev, P. 1998. "Sex on campus: A preliminary study of knowledge, attitudes and behaviour of university students in Delhi, India," *Journal of Biosocial Science,* 30 : 95-105.

Santhya, K.G. and S.J. Jejeebhoy. 2006. "Young women's experience of forced sex within marriage: Evidence from India," in *Sex without Consent: Young People in Developing Countries,* eds. S.J. Jejeebhoy, I. Shah and S. Thapa. London: Zed Books, pp. 59-73.

Santhya, K.G., N. Haberland, F. Ram *et al.* 2007. "Consent and coercion: Examining unwanted sex among married young women in India," *International Family Planning Perspectives,* 33(3): 124-32.

Santhya, K.G., S.J. Jejeebhoy and S. Ghosh. 2008. *Early Marriage and Sexual and Reproductive Health Risks: Experiences of Young Women and Men in Andhra Pradesh and Madhya Pradesh, India.* New Delhi: Population Council.

Sathar, Z.A., M. Haque, A. Faizunnissa *et al.* 2003. *Adolescents and Youth in Pakistan, 2001-02.* Islamabad: Population Council.

Sebastian, M.P., M. Grant and B. Mensch. 2005. *Integrating Adolescent Livelihood Activities Within a Reproductive Health Programme for Urban Slum Dwellers in India*. New Delhi: Population Council.

Sebastian, M.P., M. Grant, B. Mensch *et al.* 2003. *Integrating adolescent livelihood activities within a reproductive health programme for urban slum dwellers in India, Survey Questionnaire,* unpublished. New Delhi: Population Council.

Singh, S. and S. Saini. 2007. "HIV risk perception in relation to peer pressure and drug abuse behaviour among adolescents," *Indian Journal of Sexually Transmitted Diseases*, 28 : 53-54.

Srinath, S., S.C. Girimaji, G. Gururaj *et al.* 2005. "Epidemiologial study of chold and adolescent psychiatric disorders in urban and rural areas of Bangalore, India," *Indian Journal of Medical Research*, 122 : 67-79.

Sroufe, J.W. 1991. "Assessment of parent-adolescent relationships: Implications for adolescent development," *Journal of Family Psychology*, 5(1) : 21-45.

Sudan, F. 2007. Youth in Violent Conflict in Jammu and Kashmir: *A Comparative Analysis of Perceptions and Attitudes of Youth in Jammu University and Kashmir University and Migrants' Camp*. Sponsored by Centre for Study of Developing Societies, New Delhi: India.

Ul Haque, M. and A. Faizunnisa. 2003. "Access to reproductive health information in Punjab and Sindh, Pakistan: The perspectives of adolescents and parents," in *Towards Adulthood: Exploring the Sexual and Reproductive Health of Adolescents in South Asia*, eds. S. Bott, S.J. Jejeebhoy, I. Shah *et al.* Geneva: World Health Organisation, pp. 153–55.

UN Aids and Development Cooperation', Ireland, *Loc. Cit.*, Lopez P.R., *Future World Wide Health Effects of Current Smoking,* cit., in Koop E.C. and R.M. Shwarz, *Initial Issues in Global Health,* 2001, San Francisco, pp. 56-85.

UN Report on Global Aids Epidemic, 2005, Geneva, in Potdar Rukmini and Koenig A. Michael, *Does Audio–CASI Improve* Reports *of Risky Behaviour? Evidence from a Randomized field trial among Young Urban Men in India,* Jun 2005, Population Council Publication Studies in Family Planning, Vol. 36, No. 2, pp. 107-116.

United Nations Publication. 1986. *The Situation of Youth in the 1980's and Prospects and Challenges for the Year 2000.* New York, 10-11.

Verma, R.K., S. Sharma, R. Singh *et al.*, 2003. "Beliefs concerning sexual health problems and treatment seeking among men in an Indian slum community," *Culture, Health and Sexuality* 5(3): 265–76.

Wolter, K.M. 1985. *Introduction to Variance Estimation.* New York: Springer.

Yedla S.C., 1989. Youth in the Contemporary World. Mittal Publications New Delhi.

Index

Abstract principles, 47
Accidental Deaths and Suicide in India-2000, 37
Active citizenship, 118
Adolescence, 2, 11, 16, 23, 25, 27, 104, 115, 152
Adolescent Society, 24
Adulthood, 3, 8, 10–11, 13–16, 19–20, 27, 56, 85, 145, 153–55
Aggressive behaviours, 95, 124
Agriculture Department, 137
Alcohol, 5, 76, 114, 152–53
Allied activities, 67
Amenities, 91, 121
Anganwadi centers, 138
Antisocial attitudes, 28
Anti-State activities, 131
Anxiety, 36, 122–23
Arab states, 25
Aristotle, 1–2, 53
Armed conflict, 26, 115–17, 130, 147
Armed Forces Special Powers Act, 65
Aspirations and Challenges of Youth, 23
Associated Chamber of Commerce and Industry of India, 67
Assumption, 11, 18, 27, 44
Australia, 12, 16, 18–19
Awareness, 32, 75, 109, 112, 118, 147, 149, 151
Azadi campaign, 64

Bank savings account, 108–9
Behavioural characteristics, 101
Bharatiya Janata Party (BJP), 66
Bilateral agreements, 132
Biological facts, 2
Blau, Peter, 46–47
Boundary agreements, 59
Boy-girl relationship, 32, 74, 104–5
Brahmanic model, 1
Brahmin and Brahmanised caste groups, 1
Buddhists, 62, 64
Bureaucracy, 135

Caste, 120, 146, 150
  endogamy, 32
Categorical approach, 10–12, 27, 31
Central Asia and Eastern Europe, 5
Central Board of Secondary Education pattern, 70
Central Intelligence Agency, 62
Centre, 10, 133, 135
Cheap boarding houses, 129
Chenab Valley, 60
Child sex ratios, 57
Childhood, 1–3, 8–9, 12–13, 53, 70, 94
Civil society, 118, 146, 150
Class differences, 20
Coalition government, 137
Coercion, 133

Coleman's research report, 24
Community
  activities, 76
  led activities, 119, 150
  level violence, 150
Comte, August, 23
Conflict
  resolution, 128
  ridden society, 111
  situation, 115–17, 127, 147
  theory, 43–45, 50
  triggering innovation, 39
  violence, 153
Connectedness, 75
Constitution of Jammu and Kashmir, 65
Contraceptive
  methods, 75, 109, 151
  supplies, 113
Corporate Social Responsibility (CSR), 140
Cultural
  analysis, 29
  change, 23
  convention, 111
  domination, 92
  performance, 20
  studies approach, 30
  understandings, 8
Curfews, 39, 125–26

Data processing, 82
Democracy, 133
Democratic state, 26
Demographics, 57, 59, 62
Depression, 36, 122
Directive Principles of State Policy, 70
Discriminatory attitudes, 134
District Employment and Counseling Centers (DECC), 141
District level employment exchanges, 139
Domestic violence, 71, 80
Dominant culture, 29–30
Dominion of Pakistan and Union of India, 58
Drug
  abuse, 5
  addiction, 36–37, 128
  taking behaviours, 19

Economic activity, 94, 146
Education board, 70
Educational institutions, 88, 90–91, 125, 142
Emotional factors, 123
Ethnic
  conflict, 115
  Kashmiri, 64
  minority youth, 19
Ethno-regional aspirations, 134
Exchange and Reference Group Theory, 43, 46
Exchange theory, 46–47
Export Promotion Industrial Park (EPIP), 139
Extended family, 107
External factors, 130
Extracurricular activities, 126

Facebook, 127
Factionalism, 136
Feminine behaviours, 10
Femininities, 10–11, 93, 152, 154
Field
  investigators, 78
  study, 87, 96–97, 111
Fieldwork, 78–79
Forced sex, 80
Foreign exchanges, 67
Formal
  correspondences, 97–98
  education, 146
  sex, 75
Functional alternatives, 44

Gender-egalitarian child-rearing practices, 152
Gilgit-Baltistan and Azad Kashmir, 59
Giroux's analysis, 20
Growth centre, 139
Gujjars, 64, 69

Harassment, 79, 117–18, 150
Health-related activities, 81
Helplessness, 123–24
Heterogeneity, 155
HIV, 5, 75, 109
Hotel, Catering and Tourism (HCT), 129
Houseboats, 69
Human resource development, 141
Human rights abuses, 60, 127
Human rights violation, 134, 137

Income-occupational-educational groups, 55
Indian
  Army, 36, 60, 70
  military control, 62
  security forces, 38, 65, 117, 126–27
Indo-Pakistani War, 59
Industrial houses, 139
Infrastructure board, 140
Insecurity, 111, 117, 121, 123
Interactionist perspectives, 49
Interactive sessions, 78
Inter-caste marriage, 120
International Monetary Fund (IMF), 132
International Year of Youth, 9
Inter-state migration, 57

Jammu and Kashmir Employment Exchange, 139
Jammu and Kashmir Entrepreneurship Development Institute (JKEDI), 141
Jammu and Kashmir National Conference, 66
Jammu and Kashmir State Board of School Education, 70
Jammu and Kashmir State Subordinate Services Recruitment Act, 136
Johnson's analysis, 19, 27
Joint families, 32, 105, 107

Kashmir
  conflict, 116
  dispute, 133
  elections, 66
  freedom movement, 127
  Brahmins, 62
Kashmiri
  economy, 68
  Hindus, 59
  lifestyle, 69
  marriage, 111
  Pandits, 62
  saffron, 67

Labour market, 7, 15, 85, 93
Ladakh, 58–62, 64–65, 68–69
Language use, 95, 97
Late marriage, 127
Legitimate livelihood, 16–17
Life skills education programmes, 149
Low caste youth, 35

Marginalization, 28–29
Marginalized communities, 55
Marital life, 113
Marx, Karl, 44–46, 51
Masculinities, 10–11, 93, 152, 154
Mass media, 30, 36–37, 55, 98, 100, 148
Media possession, 35–36
Mental health disorders, 113, 153
Mentoring of youth, 153
Mercy Corps, 40

Ministry of Rural Development, 141
Ministry of Youth Affairs and Sports, 56
Misconceptions, 151–52
Mobile phones, 100–102
Mobilization, 24
Modernization, 32, 34–35, 55, 108, 111, 138
Mufti government, 137–38

NASA, 84
National Adolescent Reproductive and Sexual Health Strategy, 86
National Conference (NC), 65–66, 137
National Youth Policy, 56, 70, 85–86
Naya Kashmir Manifesto, 133
Nepotism, 135–36, 151
New Industrial Policy (NIP), 139
Non-Kashmiri Muslim, 64
Non-verbal correspondence, 98
Non-violent protestation, 3
Normative behaviours, 6
Nuclear families, 105–7

Opposite-sex partner, 75

Parental
  awareness, 76
  care, 105
  control, 148
  education, 84, 105
  interaction, 74
  violence, 74
Parent-child communication, 74, 104
Peer
  groups, 25, 124
  interaction, 25
People's Democratic Party (PDP), 66, 137
Physical fights, 120
Physical violence, 124
Pir Panjal range, 60–61
Plebiscite, 59
Policy implications, 145
Political agencies, 20
Political culture, 121
Political processes, 8, 17, 19, 76, 120, 150–51
Power-sharing agreement, 66
Pre-marital romantic partnerships, 75, 110
Pre-marital sex, 5, 76, 112
Pre-social self, 30
Pre-study qualitative phase, 72
Pre-survey qualitative phase, 72–73, 80
Prime Minister's Employment Guarantee Programme (PMEGP), 142
Privacy, 74, 81
Protest rallies, 127
Psychological characteristics, 27
Public resentment, 51
Public Safety Act, 39

Radical politics, 137
Recreation centers, 126
Reference groups, 47–48
Regional conflict, 115
Religious conflict, 115
Repressive character, 51
Revolutionary class conflict, 45
Romantic relationships, 72, 76, 103, 110
Rural Youth in Urban India, 34

Safe sex practices, 109
Samba and Bari Brahmna Industrial Estates, 139
Same-sex friends, 105
Sampoorna Gram Swarozgar Yojana (SGSY), 141
Save Kashmir, 40
Schooling, 7, 12, 15, 19, 74, 88, 90–91, 94, 122, 146

Secular attitudes, 76, 119, 150
Security forces (*see* Indian Security forces)
Self-efficacy, 74
Sensitive behaviours, 75, 80
Separatist campaign, 64
Sex/Sexual
  activity, 25, 54, 86, 154
  adventures, 26
  assault, 37
  composition, 86–87
  education, 109, 151, 154
  exploitation, 8, 110–11
  harassment, 111
  matters, 75, 109
  ratio, 57, 88
  relationship, 75
  roles, 9–10
  temptations, 2
  violence, 123
Sexually Transmitted Infection (STI), 75
Sher-e-Kashmir Institute of Medical Sciences, 70
Sheri-e-Kashmir Employment and Welfare Programme for Youth (SKEWPY), 142
Sheri-Kashmir Universities of Agricultural Sciences and Technology Jammu, 70
Shri Amarnath Shrine Board, 66
Siachen Glacier, 61–62
Skill development centers, 71
Social
  activity, 24
  change, 3, 9, 17, 23, 32, 44
  divisions, 15, 17, 30
  interaction, 103, 127, 148
  networking, 101, 127
  processes, 7–9, 13–14, 17
  reproduction, 3
  scientists, 4, 31, 53–54
Socialization practices, 154
Societal interests, 135
Socio-economic
  backgrounds, 34–35
  characteristics, 54
  impact of conflict on Youth, 124
Sociology of youth, 7, 26
Socio-political conflict, 55
Socio-Psychological Impact of Conflict on Youth, 122
Soft budget constraints, 133–34
Software Technology Park (STP), 139
Sovereignty, 65–66
Sports activities, 130–131
State Autonomy Committee, 135
State Financial Corporation, 136
State intervention, 18
State legislature, 65
State machinery, 136
State services, 137
Statehood, 64
Street protests, 127
Structural Functional Theory, 43
Subordinate Service Selection Board, 136
Sustainable development, 100
Symbolic value, 20–21
Symbolism of youth, 20–21
Symbolize change, 18

Territorial Constituencies, 65–66
Theoretical perspectives, 48, 50
Tobacco consumption, 114
Trans Karakoram Tract, 60

UN Resolution, 59
Unemployability, 140
United Nations Development Programme (UNDP), 132
University of Kashmir, 70
University-level education, 70
Unmarried youth, 80
Urban Aboriginal communities, 12
Urban youth, 36–38, 112–13, 142, 146

Urdu, 55, 62, 95, 97–98, 100, 106–7

Verbal communications, 97
Violent behaviours, 19
Violent conflict situation, 54
Violent conflict, 131
Vocational orientation centre, 24
Voting behaviours, 119

Wage earning activities, 148
World Trade Organization (WTO), 132

Youth
- agitations, 4
- centres, 141
- challenges, 85
- councils, 151
- development, 31
- dress, 95
- -headed households, 147
- leaders, 72
- -led summit, 39
- movements, 24
- networks, 151
- organizations, 84
- orientation, 2
- perceptions, 35, 72
- questionnaire, 73
- research, 8, 17, 31
- resource, 84
- services, 28
- skills, 147
- survey, 4, 77
- terminologies, 72
- transitions, 31
- underclass, 28–29
- uprisings, 39
- unemployed 36, 137, 139
- willingness, 72